Overcoming Burnout and Achieving Work-Life Balance

Practical Strategies for Stress Management, Mental Wellness, and Lasting Productivity

PUBLISHED BY:

MICHAEL RAYNAL

Copyright © 2024 by Michael Raynal

This is a work of nonfiction. Names, characters, businesses, places, events, and incidents are either the products of the author's imagination or used in a fictitious manner. Any resemblance to actual persons, living or dead, or actual events is purely coincidental.

First Edition: August, 2024

Dedication

To my family, for their unwavering support and love.

To my friends and colleagues, for their encouragement and belief in this project.

And to all those struggling with burnout, may you find the balance and peace you seek.

Foreword

In today's fast-paced world, where the lines between work and personal life often blur, the struggle to achieve a healthy work-life balance has become a universal challenge. As the demands of our careers grow, so too does the risk of burnout—a state of chronic physical and emotional exhaustion that leaves us feeling drained, overwhelmed, and disconnected from our passions and purpose. This book, "Overcoming Burnout and Achieving Work-Life Balance," is a beacon of hope and a practical guide for anyone navigating the tumultuous waters of modern life.

In this book, you will find a comprehensive exploration of burnout and its causes, providing you with the tools to recognize and address this pervasive issue. Understanding the multifaceted nature of burnout is the first step toward reclaiming your well-being. By identifying both personal and professional stressors, you will gain clarity on the factors that contribute to your stress and learn how to mitigate their impact.

Healthy habits and routines are the cornerstone of a balanced life. This book delves into the importance of establishing consistent daily practices that promote physical and mental health. From regular exercise and adequate sleep to mindful eating and self-care, you will discover actionable strategies to incorporate into your daily life, enhancing your overall well-being.

A robust support system is crucial in overcoming burnout. The book highlights the significance of building supportive relationships both at work and in your personal life. Whether it's communicating effectively with your manager, utilizing employee assistance programs, or seeking professional help through therapy or coaching, you will find guidance on how to foster a network of support that empowers you to thrive.

Creating a balanced work environment is another key focus of this book. You will learn how to redesign your workday to include flexible arrangements, promote a healthy workplace culture, and set clear boundaries to manage work-related stress. These practical steps will help you cultivate an environment where productivity and well-being coexist harmoniously.

Enhancing personal well-being extends beyond the workplace. This book encourages you to pursue hobbies and interests that bring joy and fulfillment, emphasizing the benefits of creative outlets and personal passions. Maintaining a healthy lifestyle through regular exercise and nutritious choices is also covered, offering you a holistic approach to well-being.

Implementing work-life balance practices requires a thoughtful and personalized plan. You will be guided on how to create a work-life balance plan that sets clear boundaries, allocates time for personal activities, and aligns your career ambitions with your personal values. Regularly reviewing and adjusting your goals will ensure that your plan remains effective and relevant.

Real-life success stories featured in this book provide inspiration and practical insights. By learning from individuals and organizations that have successfully navigated burnout and achieved work-life balance, you will gain valuable perspectives and motivation to apply these lessons to your own life. Expert insights and advice from professionals in mental health and work-life balance add depth to the narrative, offering you well-rounded guidance.

To support your journey, the book concludes with a rich collection of tools and resources. An essential reading list, online resources, apps, workshops, and interactive tools are provided to help you manage stress and maintain balance. Quizzes and assessments included in the book will assist you in identifying areas for improvement and tracking your progress.

As you embark on this journey of self-discovery and transformation, remember that achieving work-life balance is an ongoing process. Be patient with yourself, celebrate your successes, and stay committed to your well-being. This book is not just a guide but a companion, offering you the wisdom, tools, and encouragement to create a balanced, fulfilling life.

Welcome to "Overcoming Burnout and Achieving Work-Life Balance." May this book be a catalyst for positive change in your life, empowering you to thrive both personally and professionally.

Table of Contents

Introduction

Defining Burnout and Work-Life Balance

Burnout is a state of physical, emotional, and mental exhaustion that results from prolonged exposure to stressful work environments or demanding personal circumstances. It is characterized by a lack of motivation, decreased productivity, and a sense of detachment from one's work or personal life. Burnout is often described as a state of emotional, physical, and mental depletion, where an individual feels overwhelmed, drained, and unable to cope with the demands placed upon them.

On the other hand, work-life balance refers to the ability to maintain a healthy equilibrium between the demands of one's job and the needs of their personal life. It involves prioritizing and allocating time and energy between work responsibilities and personal pursuits, such as family, hobbies, and self-care activities. Achieving a work-life balance is crucial for maintaining overall well-being, as it helps to prevent burnout, improve job satisfaction, and foster a sense of fulfillment in both professional and personal spheres.

Why This Book Matters

The Impact of Burnout can have far-reaching consequences on an individual's well-being, productivity, and overall quality of life. It can lead to decreased job satisfaction, strained relationships, and even physical health issues such as chronic fatigue, headaches, and cardiovascular problems.

In the workplace, burnout can result in increased absenteeism, high turnover rates, and reduced organizational efficiency, leading to significant financial and operational challenges for employers. The impact of burnout extends beyond the individual, as it can also have ripple effects on families, communities, and society as a whole.

When individuals are unable to manage their stress and maintain a healthy work-life balance, it can lead to a decline in their overall mental and physical health, which can negatively impact their ability to fulfill their personal and professional responsibilities.

This, in turn, can strain relationships, disrupt family dynamics, and contribute to a broader societal issue of diminished well-being and productivity.

This book aims to provide readers with practical strategies and insights to overcome burnout and achieve a sustainable work-life balance, ultimately improving their overall well-being and professional success. By addressing the root causes of burnout and equipping readers with effective coping mechanisms, the book seeks to empower individuals to take control of their lives, enhance their productivity and job satisfaction, and foster a greater sense of fulfillment in both their work and personal pursuits.

How to Use This Book

A Guide for Readers this book is designed to be a comprehensive guide for individuals struggling with burnout or seeking to maintain a healthy work-life balance. Readers will find a step-by-step approach to understanding the root causes of burnout, developing personalized coping mechanisms, and implementing sustainable lifestyle changes. Each chapter will offer a mix of theoretical knowledge, real-life examples, and actionable steps to help readers navigate their unique challenges and embark on a journey towards a more fulfilling and balanced life.

The content is structured in a way that allows readers to build a solid foundation of understanding, followed by practical strategies and tools they can immediately apply to their own lives. Throughout the book, readers will be encouraged to engage in self-reflection, identify their personal burnout triggers, and develop a customized plan for overcoming burnout and achieving work-life balance.

The book will also feature inspiring stories and case studies of individuals who have successfully navigated the challenges of burnout, offering readers a sense of hope and motivation as they work towards their own goals. By following the guidance and recommendations provided in this book, readers will be empowered to take control of their lives, prioritize their well-being, and find a sustainable balance between their professional and personal responsibilities. Whether you are a busy executive, a caregiver juggling multiple roles, or an individual simply seeking to improve your overall quality of life, this book will serve as a valuable resource to help you overcome burnout and thrive in all aspects of your life.

Chapter One

Understanding Burnout

What is Burnout?

Burnout is a state of emotional, physical, and mental exhaustion that can occur when an individual experiences prolonged stress or demands that exceed their coping abilities. It is often characterized by a sense of detachment, a lack of motivation, and a decreased sense of accomplishment. Burnout can manifest in various ways, including physical symptoms, cognitive impairment, and emotional distress. The concept of burnout was first introduced in the 1970s by the American psychologist Herbert Freudenberger, who observed that healthcare professionals and social workers were experiencing a particular form of work-related stress that led to a profound sense of emotional and physical depletion. Since then, the understanding of burnout has evolved, and it is now recognized as a widespread phenomenon that can affect individuals in a wide range of professions and personal circumstances. Burnout is not a temporary state of fatigue or stress; it is a chronic condition that develops gradually over time, often without the individual even realizing the extent of the problem.

The gradual nature of burnout can make it particularly insidious, as it can creep up on individuals who are initially highly motivated and engaged in their work or personal pursuits.

Symptoms and Signs

The symptoms of burnout can vary from person to person, but they often include a combination of physical, emotional, and behavioral manifestations. Some of the most common symptoms and signs of burnout include:

Physical Symptoms:- Chronic fatigue and lack of energy- Headaches, muscle tension, or other physical aches and pains- Digestive issues, such as stomach problems or changes in appetite- Weakened immune system, leading to more frequent illnesses.

Emotional Symptoms:- Cynicism and a negative attitude towards work or personal life- Feelings of helplessness, hopelessness, or detachment- Irritability, anxiety, or depression- Decreased sense of accomplishment or self-worth.

Behavioral Symptoms:-

- Decreased productivity and performance

- Difficulty concentrating or making decisions

- Withdrawal from social activities or interpersonal relationships

- Increased use of unhealthy coping mechanisms, such as substance abuse or overeating.

It's important to note that the presence of one or more of these symptoms does not necessarily indicate burnout, as they can also be associated with other health conditions or life stressors. However, the persistent and pervasive nature of these symptoms, combined with a sense of emotional and physical depletion, is a clear indication that an individual may be experiencing burnout.

Causes and Triggers

Burnout can be triggered by a variety of factors, both in the workplace and in one's personal life. Some of the most common causes and triggers of burnout include:

Work-Related Factors:

- Excessive workload or long work hours

- Lack of control or autonomy over job responsibilities

- Unclear job expectations or role ambiguity

- Lack of support or recognition from supervisors or colleagues

- Emotionally demanding work, such as dealing with difficult clients or patients- Lack of work-life balance, with little time for rest and relaxation.

Personal Life Influences

- Relationship conflicts or difficulties

- Financial stress or instability

- Caring for family members, such as young children or elderly parents

- Major life events or transitions, such as a move, divorce, or the loss of a loved one

- Unhealthy lifestyle habits, such as poor sleep, diet, or exercise- Lack of time for self-care and leisure activities.

It's important to recognize that burnout is not solely a work-related issue; it can also be triggered by personal life factors or a combination of both. The unique circumstances and experiences of each individual can contribute to the development of burnout, making it a highly personalized phenomenon.

The Science Behind Burnout

Burnout is a complex phenomenon that involves both psychological and physiological processes. At its core, burnout is a result of the body's stress response mechanism being overwhelmed and unable to recover properly.

Stress Response Mechanisms

When faced with a stressful situation, the body's sympathetic nervous system is activated, triggering the release of hormones like cortisol and adrenaline. This "fight-or-flight" response is designed to help the body cope with immediate threats. However, when the stress response is prolonged, as in the case of chronic burnout, it can have detrimental effects on both mental and physical health.

The prolonged activation of the stress response system can lead to a depletion of the body's resources, as the individual is constantly in a state of heightened arousal. This can result in a range of physiological changes, including increased heart rate, elevated blood pressure, and a weakened immune system. Over time, these physiological changes can contribute to the development of various health problems, both physical and mental.

Long-Term Effects on Mental and Physical Health

Prolonged exposure to stress and burnout can lead to a variety of long-term health consequences, including:

Mental Health Impacts

- Increased risk of mental health issues such as depression, anxiety, and post-traumatic stress disorder

- Impaired cognitive function, including difficulty with memory, concentration, and decision-making- Emotional exhaustion and a decreased sense of personal accomplishment.

Physical Health Impacts

- Weakened immune system, making individuals more susceptible to illness

- Cardiovascular problems, such as high blood pressure and an increased risk of heart disease.

- Gastrointestinal issues, such as digestive problems and irritable bowel syndrome- Musculoskeletal problems, including chronic pain and tension headaches

- Disruptions to the body's sleep-wake cycle and overall sleep quality.

These long-term effects of burnout can have a significant impact on an individual's quality of life, as they can interfere with their ability to function effectively in both their personal and professional spheres. Understanding the science behind burnout is crucial for developing effective strategies to overcome this challenge and restore a healthy work-life balance.

Identifying Your Personal Burnout Triggers

Recognizing the specific factors that contribute to your burnout is the first step in developing effective coping strategies. Burnout triggers can be found both in the workplace and in one's personal life, and it's important to take the time to reflect on and identify the unique circumstances that are contributing to your feelings of emotional, physical, and mental exhaustion.

Work-Related Factors

 In the workplace, some of the most common burnout triggers include:-

-Excessive workload or unrealistic deadlines: When the demands of the job exceed an individual's capacity to manage them, it can lead to a sense of being overwhelmed and unable to keep up.

- Lack of control or autonomy over job responsibilities: Feeling like you have little or no say in how your work is organized or prioritized can contribute to a sense of powerlessness and frustration.

- Poor work-life balance, with long hours and limited time for rest and relaxation: A lack of balance between work and personal life can lead to burnout, as individuals struggle to maintain their energy and focus.

- Lack of support or recognition from supervisors or colleagues: Feeling undervalued or unsupported in the workplace can erode an individual's sense of purpose and motivation.

- Unclear job expectations or role ambiguity: When an individual is unsure of their responsibilities or the expectations placed upon them, it can create a sense of uncertainty and stress.

- Emotionally demanding work, such as caring for patients or clients: Professions that require a high level of emotional investment can be particularly susceptible to burnout, as the constant need to empathize and provide support can be draining.

Personal Life Influences

Burnout can also be triggered by factors outside of the workplace, such as:

- Relationship conflicts or difficulties: Strained personal relationships, whether with a partner, family members, or friends, can contribute to emotional and mental exhaustion.

- Financial stress or instability: Worries about money and financial security can add to an individual's overall stress levels and sense of lack of control.- Caring for family members, such as young children or elderly parents: The demands of caregiving, especially when combined with work responsibilities, can be a significant source of burnout.

- Major life events or transitions, such as a move, divorce, or the loss of a loved one: Significant life changes can disrupt an individual's sense of stability and contribute to feelings of overwhelm.

- Unhealthy lifestyle habits, such as poor sleep, diet, or exercise: Neglecting self-care can exacerbate the symptoms of burnout and make it more difficult to cope.

- Lack of time for self-care and leisure activities: When individuals do not prioritize their own well-being and make time for activities that replenish their energy and restore their sense of balance, it can lead to burnout. By identifying the specific factors that contribute to your burnout, you can develop a more personalized approach to addressing the problem and implementing strategies for achieving a sustainable work-life balance. This self-awareness is a crucial first step in your journey towards overcoming burnout and reclaiming your overall well-being.

Chapter Two

Assessing Your Current Situation

Burnout and an unbalanced life can creep up slowly, often going unnoticed until they reach a critical point. Before you can take steps to overcome burnout and achieve a healthier work-life balance, it's essential to assess your current situation thoroughly.

This chapter will guide you through various self-assessment tools, help you evaluate your work-life balance, and assist you in setting realistic goals.

Self-Assessment Tools

To begin addressing burnout, you need a clear understanding of where you stand. Self-assessment tools can provide valuable insights into your stress levels, workload, and overall well-being.

Questionnaires and Checklists

Questionnaires and checklists are effective ways to assess your current situation. These tools can help you identify symptoms of burnout and areas of your life that may be out of balance.

Here are a few examples:

- **Burnout Inventory:** This tool measures the extent of your burnout. It includes questions about emotional exhaustion, depersonalization, and personal accomplishment.

- **Work-Life Balance Scale:** This scale assesses how well you balance work demands with personal life. It considers factors like time spent at work, satisfaction with work-life balance, and the impact of work on personal relationships.

- **Stress Assessment:** This tool evaluates your stress levels based on physical, emotional, and behavioral symptoms. It can help you identify stressors and their severity.

Professional Assessments

While self-assessment tools are valuable for gaining initial insights into your burnout and stress levels, professional assessments can provide a more comprehensive and nuanced understanding of your situation. Mental health professionals and career coaches are equipped with the expertise and experience to offer personalized insights and recommendations that are tailored to your specific circumstances.

The Role of Mental Health

Professionals

Mental health professionals, such as psychologists, therapists, and counselors, can help you delve deeper into the emotional and psychological aspects of burnout. They use various diagnostic tools and therapeutic techniques to identify the root causes of your stress and burnout. Through structured sessions, these professionals can help you:

1. **Identify Underlying Issues**: Mental health professionals can uncover underlying issues such as anxiety, depression, or unresolved trauma that may be contributing to your burnout. Addressing these issues is crucial for achieving long-term well-being.

2. **Develop Coping Strategies**: They can teach you effective coping strategies to manage stress, such as cognitive-behavioral techniques, mindfulness practices, and relaxation exercises. These strategies can help you build resilience and prevent future burnout.

3. **Create a Treatment Plan**: Based on their assessments, mental health professionals can create a tailored treatment plan that includes therapy, lifestyle changes, and possibly medication if needed. This holistic approach ensures that all aspects of your well-being are addressed.

The Role of Career Coaches

Career coaches, on the other hand, focus on the professional aspects of your life. They help you navigate career challenges, enhance your job satisfaction, and align your professional goals with your personal values. Here's how career coaches can assist you:

1. **Clarify Career Goals**: Career coaches can help you clarify your career goals and aspirations. They assist you in identifying what truly matters to you in your professional life, whether it's job satisfaction, career advancement, work-life balance, or financial stability.

2. **Improve Work Efficiency**: They can provide strategies to improve your work efficiency and productivity. This includes time management techniques, prioritization methods, and skills development to help you handle your workload more effectively.

3. **Navigate Career Transitions**: If you are considering a career change or transition, career coaches can guide you through the process. They offer insights into different career paths, help you update your resume, and prepare you for job interviews.

Combining Both Approaches

For a holistic approach to overcoming burnout, consider combining the expertise of both mental health professionals and career coaches. This integrated approach addresses both the emotional and professional aspects of your life, providing a well-rounded support system.

Evaluating Your Work-Life Balance

After gaining a clearer understanding of your burnout and stress levels through both self-assessments and professional evaluations, the next step is to evaluate your work-life balance. This involves a thorough analysis of your workload, personal time, and priorities to identify areas for improvement.

Workload Analysis

A critical component of evaluating your work-life balance is analyzing your workload. This involves taking a detailed inventory of all your professional responsibilities, including tasks, projects, and deadlines. Here's a step-by-step guide to conducting a workload analysis:

1. **List Your Responsibilities**: Start by listing every task, project, and responsibility you have at work. Be honest and comprehensive. Include both major projects and minor tasks.

2. **Categorize Your Tasks**: Once you have a complete list, categorize each item based on its importance and urgency. Use the following categories:

    o **High Importance/High Urgency**: These tasks require immediate attention and are crucial to your role. They often have tight deadlines and significant consequences if not completed on time.

    o **High Importance/Low Urgency**: These tasks are important but do not need immediate attention. They can be scheduled for later, allowing you to plan and allocate sufficient time to complete them.

    o **Low Importance/High Urgency**: These tasks demand immediate attention but are not crucial. Consider delegating these tasks to others or finding ways to minimize their impact on your workload.

- o **Low Importance/Low Urgency**: These tasks are neither important nor urgent. They can often be eliminated, postponed, or performed during downtime.

3. **Evaluate and Adjust**: After categorizing your tasks, evaluate how much time you are spending on each category. Aim to reduce the time spent on low importance tasks and reallocate that time to high importance tasks. This helps you focus on what truly matters and improves your overall productivity.

Balancing Personal Time and Priorities

Beyond workload analysis, it's essential to evaluate how you are balancing your personal time and priorities. Consider the following steps:

1. **Identify Personal Priorities**: Reflect on what is most important to you outside of work. This could include family, friends, hobbies, health,

or personal development. Write down your top personal priorities.

2. **Analyze Time Allocation**: Track how you currently spend your time each day. Identify any discrepancies between your priorities and where your time is actuallygoing. Are you spending enough time on activities that matter to you?

3. **Set Boundaries**: Establish clear boundaries between work and personal life. This might mean setting specific work hours, turning off work notifications after a certain time, or designating certain days for personal activities.

4. **Schedule Personal Time**: Just as you schedule work tasks, schedule time for your personal priorities. Treat these appointments with the same importance as work meetings to ensure they are not overlooked.

Creating a Balanced Schedule

By analyzing your workload and balancing your personal time and priorities, you can create a more balanced schedule. Here are some additional tips:

- **Use a Planner**: Use a planner or digital calendar to organize your tasks and personal activities. This helps you visualize your schedule and ensures you allocate time for both work and personal life.

- **Prioritize Self-Care**: Make self-care a non-negotiable part of your routine. This includes regular exercise, healthy eating, adequate sleep, and relaxation activities.

- **Seek Flexibility**: If possible, seek flexible work arrangements that allow you to better balance your professional and personal life. This could include remote work, flexible hours, or job sharing.

In conclusion, evaluating your work-life balance involves a comprehensive analysis of your workload, personal time, and priorities. By understanding and addressing these areas, you can reduce stress, prevent burnout, and create a more fulfilling and balanced life.

Personal Time and Priorities

Balancing your workload is only part of the equation. You must also evaluate how you spend your personal time and whether it aligns with your priorities. Reflect on the following questions:

- How much time do you dedicate to work outside of regular hours?

- Are you spending enough time with family and friends?

- Do you engage in activities that bring you joy and relaxation?

- Are you taking care of your physical and mental health?

By answering these questions, you can identify areas where you need to make changes to achieve a better work-life balance.

Setting Realistic Goals

Setting realistic goals is a crucial step in overcoming burnout and achieving work-life balance. With a clear understanding of your current situation—gained through self-assessments, professional evaluations, and workload analysis—you can now chart a path forward that is both achievable and sustainable. To ensure your goals are effective, they should be specific, measurable, achievable, relevant, and time-bound (SMART).

This approach provides a structured framework that enhances your chances of success.

Specific

Your goals should be clear and specific, leaving no room for ambiguity. A well-defined goal provides direction and focus, making it easier to understand what you need to do to achieve it. When setting specific goals, consider the following questions:

- What exactly do I want to accomplish?

- Why is this goal important?

- Who is involved?

- Where is it located?

- Which resources or limits are involved**?**

Example: Instead of setting a vague goal like "reduce stress," make it specific: "Practice mindfulness meditation for 15 minutes every morning to reduce stress."

Measurable

Measurable goals help you track your progress and stay motivated. By setting criteria for measuring your progress, you can determine if you're on track to reach your goal. When setting measurable goals, ask yourself:

- How much?

- How many?

- How will I know when it is accomplished?

Example: "Exercise for at least 30 minutes, five times a week" is a measurable goal. You can easily track the number of workouts per week and the duration of each session.

Achievable

Your goals should be realistic and attainable. While it's important to challenge yourself, setting goals that are too ambitious can lead to frustration and burnout. Consider your current resources, skills, and constraints when setting achievable goals. Reflect on the following:

- How can I accomplish this goal?

- What resources or support do I need?

- Is this goal attainable within the given constraints?

Example: If you are new to meditation, starting with a goal of meditating for one hour every day may not be achievable. Instead, begin with 10-15 minutes daily and gradually increase the duration as you become more comfortable with the practice.

Relevant

Your goals should align with your broader objectives and values. Ensuring that your goals are relevant helps you stay focused on what truly matters to you and prevents you from getting sidetracked by less important tasks. Ask yourself:

- Is this goal worthwhile?

- Is this the right time?

- Does this goal align with my other goals?

- Is this goal relevant to my long-term objectives?

Example: If achieving a better work-life balance is a priority, a relevant goal might be "leave work by 6 PM at least three times a week to spend quality time with family."

Time-bound

Every goal needs a target date to focus on and a deadline to work towards. Time-bound goals create a sense of urgency and help you prioritize your tasks. Consider the following:

- When?

- What can I do six months from now?

- What can I do six weeks from now?

- What can I do today?

Example: "Complete a professional development course on stress management within the next three months" is a time-bound goal. The deadline helps you stay focused and ensures that you allocate time to complete the course.

Putting SMART Goals into Practice

Let's put the SMART framework into practice with a step-by-step example related to achieving work-life balance:

1. **Identify the Issue**: You feel overwhelmed by work and want to improve your work-life balance.

2. **Set a Specific Goal**: "Reduce work-related stress by incorporating daily exercise."

3. **Make it Measurable**: "Exercise for at least 30 minutes, five times a week."

4. **Ensure it's Achievable**: "I will start with brisk walking or yoga, activities that I enjoy and can easily fit into my schedule."

5. **Keep it Relevant**: "Improving my physical health will help me manage stress better and achieve a healthier work-life balance."

6. **Set a Time-bound Target**: "I will begin this routine next Monday and aim to maintain it for the next three months, reviewing my progress at the end of each month."

Illustrations

1. **Scenario Illustration**: Imagine Jane, a marketing manager, feeling overwhelmed by her workload and struggling to find time for her personal life. Using the SMART framework, she sets the following goal:

   o **Specific**: Jane wants to improve her physical health to manage stress better.

   o **Measurable**: She decides to exercise for 30 minutes, five times a week.

   o **Achievable**: Jane chooses activities she enjoys, such as running and yoga, to ensure she sticks to her routine.

   o **Relevant**: By improving her health, Jane expects to have more energy and a better mindset to handle work challenges.

- **Time-bound**: Jane sets a three-month target to establish this routine and reviews her progress monthly.

2. **Visualization Tool**: Use a goal-setting worksheet to break down your goals. Here's a simple template:

Goal	Description
Specific	What exactly do I want to achieve?
Measurable	How will I track my progress?
Achievable	Is this goal realistic given my current resources and constraints?
Relevant	How does this goal align with my broader objectives and values?

Goal	Description
Time-bound	What is my deadline for achieving this goal?
Action Steps	What steps will I take to achieve this goal?
Potential Obstacles	What challenges might I face, and how will I address them?
Support Needed	Who can support me in achieving this goal?

3. By filling out this worksheet, you can ensure that each goal is well-defined and actionable.

Benefits of SMART Goals

Setting SMART goals offers several benefits:

- **Clarity**: Clear and specific goals provide direction and focus.

- **Motivation**: Measurable goals allow you to track progress and stay motivated.

- **Feasibility**: Achievable goals ensure you don't set yourself up for failure.

- **Relevance**: Relevant goals keep you aligned with your long-term objectives.

- **Urgency**: Time-bound goals create a sense of urgency and help you prioritize your efforts.

Setting realistic goals using the SMART framework is a powerful strategy for overcoming burnout and achieving work-life balance. By ensuring your goals are specific, measurable, achievable, relevant, and time-bound, you can create a clear roadmap to success. This structured approach not only helps you stay focused and motivated but also ensures that your efforts are aligned with your broader objectives and values. Remember, the journey to achieving work-life balance is ongoing, and regularly revisiting and adjusting your goals is key to maintaining a healthy and fulfilling life.

Short-Term and Long-Term Objectives

Break down your goals into short-term and long-term objectives. Short-term objectives are immediate actions you can take to relieve stress and improve balance. Long-term objectives focus on sustainable changes that will benefit you over time.

Short-Term Objectives:

- Take regular breaks throughout the day to recharge.

- Set boundaries for work hours and stick to them.

- Practice mindfulness or meditation for a few minutes daily.

- Delegate tasks where possible.

Long-Term Objectives:

- Develop a comprehensive time management plan.

- Build a strong support network of family, friends, and colleagues.

- Pursue hobbies and interests outside of work.

- Maintain a healthy lifestyle through exercise, nutrition, and sleep.

Measuring Progress

It's important to regularly measure your progress toward

your goals. Keep a journal or use a tracking app to document your achievements and setbacks. Reflect on what is working and what needs adjustment. This ongoing assessment will help you stay on track and make necessary changes to your plan.

Chapter Three

Strategies for Overcoming Burnout

Now that you have assessed your current situation and set realistic goals, it's time to explore strategies for overcoming burnout. This chapter provides immediate relief techniques, long-term strategies, and guidance on creating a personal wellness plan.

Immediate Relief Techniques

Burnout can feel overwhelming, but finding immediate relief is possible with the right techniques. These methods help manage stress and prevent it from escalating, offering both short-term comfort and long-term benefits. Here are some effective strategies to consider:

Breathing Exercises and Meditation

Breathing exercises and meditation are powerful tools for calming the mind and reducing stress. These techniques can be easily incorporated into your daily routine and require no special equipment. Here are a few simple yet effective methods:

Deep Breathing

Deep breathing is one of the most straightforward and effective ways to calm the nervous system. It helps oxygenate the blood and promotes a sense of relaxation.

1. **Find a Comfortable Position**: Sit or lie down in a comfortable position. Close your eyes if it helps you focus.

2. **Inhale Deeply**: Take a deep breath in through your nose, allowing your abdomen to expand fully. Imagine filling your lungs from the bottom up.

3. **Hold the Breath**: Hold the breath for a few seconds. This helps maximize the oxygen exchange.

4. **Exhale Slowly**: Exhale slowly through your mouth, letting all the air out completely.

Imagine pushing the stress and tension out with your breath.

5. **Repeat**: Repeat this process several times, focusing on the breath and the sensations in your body.

Progressive Muscle Relaxation

Progressive muscle relaxation (PMR) involves tensing and then relaxing different muscle groups in the body. This technique can  help reduce physical tension and promote relaxation.

1. **Get Comfortable**: Find a quiet place where you won't be disturbed. Sit or lie down comfortably.

2. **Start with Your Toes**: Begin by tensing the muscles in your toes. Hold the tension for about five seconds.

3. **Release**: Slowly release the tension and notice the difference in how your muscles feel.

4. **Move Up Your Body**: Progressively move up your body, tensing and then relaxing each muscle group. Go from your feet to your calves, thighs, abdomen, chest, arms, and finally, your face.

5. **Focus on the Sensation**: Pay attention to the sensation of relaxation spreading through your body as you release each muscle group.

Mindfulness Meditation

Mindfulness meditation involves focusing on the present moment and observing your thoughts and feelings without judgment. This practice can help you develop a greater sense of awareness and control over your mind.

1. **Find a Quiet Space**: Choose a quiet place where you can sit comfortably without distractions.

2. **Focus on Your Breath**: Close your eyes and focus on your breath. Notice the sensation of the air entering and leaving your nostrils.

3. **Observe Your Thoughts**: As you meditate, you may find that your mind starts to wander. This is normal. When it happens, gently bring your focus back to your breath.

4. **Be Present**: Try to stay present in the moment, observing your thoughts and feelings without getting caught up in them.

5. **Practice Regularly**: Even a few minutes of mindfulness meditation each day can have a significant impact on your stress levels.

Short Breaks and Quick Wins

Incorporating short breaks and quick wins into your daily routine can help prevent burnout and improve your overall well-being. These small actions can make a big difference in how you feel throughout the day.

Stretching

Sitting for long periods can cause physical tension and discomfort. Taking a few minutes to stretch can help release tension and improve your posture.

1. **Stand Up**: Stand up and reach your arms overhead, stretching your entire body.

2. **Neck Stretches**: Gently tilt your head to one side, bringing your ear towards your shoulder. Hold for a few seconds, then switch sides.

3. **Shoulder Rolls**: Roll your shoulders forward and backward to release tension.

4. **Hamstring Stretch**: While standing, bend at the waist and reach for your toes, stretching your hamstrings.

Walks

Taking a short walk outside can clear your mind, boost your mood, and provide a change of scenery.

Aim for at least a few minutes of walking every day.

1. **Find a Nearby Path**: Choose a safe and pleasant path for your walk, whether it's around your neighborhood, a park, or even your office building.

2. **Breathe Fresh Air**: As you walk, take deep breaths and enjoy the fresh air.

3. **Observe Your Surroundings**: Pay attention to the sights, sounds, and smells around you. This can help you stay present and mindful during your walk.

Mini-Meditation

Even a few minutes of meditation can help you reset and refocus. Try incorporating mini-meditation sessions into your day.

1. **Find a Quiet Spot**: Choose a quiet place where you can sit comfortably.

2. **Focus on Your Breath**: Close your eyes and focus on your breath for a few minutes.

3. **Set a Timer**: Use a timer to remind yourself to take these mini-meditation breaks throughout the day.

Long-Term Strategies

While immediate relief techniques are valuable, achieving lasting change requires addressing the root causes of burnout. Long-term strategies focus on time management, prioritization, delegation, and creating a comprehensive wellness plan.

Time Management and Prioritization

Effective time management is essential for reducing stress and preventing burnout. Here are some strategies to help you manage your time more effectively:

Create a Daily Schedule

A well-structured daily schedule can help you stay organized and ensure you allocate time for both work and personal activities.

1. **Plan Your Day**: At the start of each day, list your tasks and prioritize them based on importance and urgency.

2. **Set Time Blocks**: Allocate specific time blocks for different tasks and activities. Be realistic about how much time each task will take.

3. **Include Breaks**: Schedule regular breaks to rest and recharge. This can help you maintain your energy levels throughout the day.

Prioritize Tasks

1. Prioritizing tasks helps you focus on what truly matters and avoid getting overwhelmed by less important activities:

1. Identify Key Tasks: Determine which tasks are most important and align with your long-term goals.

2. **Use the Eisenhower Matrix**: The Eisenhower Matrix is a useful tool for prioritizing tasks based on their importance and urgency. Categorize tasks into four quadrants:

   - **Urgent and Important**: Do these tasks first.

   - **Important but Not Urgent**: Schedule these tasks.

   - **Urgent but Not Important**: Delegate these tasks if possible.

o **Neither Urgent nor Important**: Consider eliminating or postponing these tasks.

Set Realistic Deadlines

Setting realistic deadlines helps you manage your workload and reduces the pressure to complete everything at once.

1. **Break Tasks into Smaller Steps**: Large tasks can be overwhelming. Break them down into smaller, more manageable steps.

2. **Set Incremental Deadlines**: Assign deadlines for each step, ensuring they are realistic and achievable.

Delegation and Saying No

Delegating tasks can help lighten your workload and free up time for activities that require your unique skills and expertise.

Identify Tasks to Delegate

Determine which tasks can be delegated to others, allowing you to focus on more critical responsibilities.

1. **Routine Tasks**: Delegate routine tasks that do not require your specific expertise.

2. **Tasks Others Can Do Better**: Delegate tasks that others are better equipped to handle or that fall within their area of expertise.

Choose the Right People

Select the right people to delegate tasks to, ensuring they have the necessary skills and resources.

1. **Assess Skills**: Consider the skills and capabilities of your team members.

2. **Provide Clear Instructions**: Clearly communicate what needs to be done and provide any necessary resources or support.

Monitor Progress

While delegating tasks, it's important to monitor progress and provide feedback to ensure tasks are completed effectively.

1. **Set Check-In Points**: Schedule regular check-ins to review progress and address any issues.

2. **Offer Support**: Be available to provide guidance and support as needed.

Key Summary

Learning to delegate and say no is crucial for managing your workload.

- **Identify Tasks that can be delegated:** Review your tasks and identify those that can be delegated to others. This frees up your time for more important responsibilities.

- **Communicate Clearly:** When delegating, provide clear instructions and expectations to ensure tasks are completed effectively.

- **Set Boundaries:** Learn to say no to additional tasks or commitments that may overload your schedule. Prioritize your well-being over taking on too much.

Creating a Wellness Plan

A comprehensive wellness plan addresses all aspects of your well-being, including physical, emotional, and mental health. Here's how to create an effective wellness plan:

Assess Your Current Wellness

Evaluate your current wellness in various areas to identify areas for improvement.

Integrating Physical Activity

1. **Physical Health**: Consider your exercise routine, diet, sleep habits, and any health concerns.

2. **Emotional Health**: Reflect on your emotional well-being, stress levels, and coping mechanisms.

3. **Mental Health**: Assess your mental health, including any symptoms of anxiety, depression, or burnout.

Set Wellness Goals

Based on your assessment, set specific, measurable, achievable, relevant, and time-bound (SMART) wellness goals.

1. **Physical Health Goals**: Set goals related to exercise, nutrition, and sleep. For example, aim to exercise for 30 minutes a day, five times a week.

2. **Emotional Health Goals**: Set goals to improve emotional well-being, such as practicing mindfulness or seeking therapy.

3. **Mental Health Goals**: Set goals to support mental health, such as reducing work-related stress or improving work-life balance.

Create an Action Plan

Develop a detailed action plan to achieve your wellness goals.

1. **Identify Steps**: Outline the specific steps needed to achieve each goal.

2. **Set Deadlines**: Assign deadlines for each step to keep yourself on track.

3. **Seek Support**: Identify resources and support systems that can help you achieve your goals, such as fitness classes, counseling, or support groups.

Monitor and Adjust

Regularly monitor your progress and make adjustments to your wellness plan as needed.

1. **Track Progress**: Keep a journal or use an app to track your progress towards your wellness goals.

2. **Evaluate and Adjust**: Periodically evaluate your plan and make adjustments based on what's working and what's not.

Immediate relief techniques and long-term strategies are both essential for managing burnout and achieving a sustainable work-life balance. By incorporating breathing exercises, meditation, short breaks, and quick wins into your daily routine, you can find immediate relief from stress. Additionally, by focusing on time management, prioritization, delegation, and creating a comprehensive wellness plan, you can address the root causes of burnout and achieve lasting change. Remember, the journey to overcoming burnout and achieving work-life balance is ongoing. Regularly revisiting and adjusting your strategies is key to maintaining a healthy and fulfilling life.

Developing Healthy Eating Habits

Nutrition plays a significant role in your overall well-being. Here are some tips for healthy eating:

- **Balanced Diet:** Ensure your diet includes a variety of fruits, vegetables, whole grains, lean proteins, and healthy fats.

- **Mindful Eating:** Pay attention to your eating habits, savor your food, and avoid distractions while eating.

- **Hydration:** Drink plenty of water throughout the day to stay hydrated and maintain energy levels.

Ensuring Adequate Sleep

Sleep is critical for physical and mental health. Here's how to improve your sleep:

- **Sleep Schedule:** Establish a consistent sleep schedule by going to bed and waking up at the same time each day.

- **Sleep Environment:** Create a restful sleep environment by keeping your bedroom cool, dark, and quiet.

- **Relaxation Techniques:** Practice relaxation techniques, such as reading or gentle stretching, before bed to prepare your body and mind for sleep.

By incorporating these long-term strategies into your daily routine, you can effectively manage stress, prevent burnout, and achieve a better work-life balance.

Chapter Four

Building a Support System

Burnout is not something that you have to face alone. Building a strong support system is crucial for overcoming burnout and maintaining a healthy work-life balance. This chapter will guide you on finding support at work, strengthening personal relationships, and seeking professional help.

Finding Support at Work

Your workplace can be a significant source of support if you know where to look and how to ask for it.

Communicating with Your Manager

Open communication with your manager is vital for addressing burnout.

Here are some steps to ensure effective communication:

- **Schedule a Meeting:** Request a dedicated time to discuss your concerns. Make it clear that you need uninterrupted time to have an in-depth conversation.

- **Be Honest and Specific:** Clearly articulate the issues you're facing. Use specific examples to illustrate how your workload or workplace environment is contributing to your burnout.

- **Propose Solutions:** Don't just present problems; come with potential solutions. This could include flexible work hours, reducing your workload, or reassigning certain tasks.

- **Follow-Up:** Ensure there is a follow-up plan to review the changes and their impact. Regular check-ins can help keep the communication lines open and adjustments can be made as needed.

Utilizing Employee Assistance Programs

Employee Assistance Programs (EAPs) are a valuable resource provided by many organizations to support the well-being of their employees. These programs offer a range of services designed to help employees manage personal and professional challenges, thereby enhancing their overall health and productivity. Here's a detailed exploration of how to effectively utilize EAPs:

Explore Available Resources

Familiarize Yourself with Offerings`

The first step in utilizing EAPs is to familiarize yourself with what your program offers. EAPs can provide a variety of services, including:

- **Counseling Services**: These can address issues such as stress, anxiety, depression, relationship problems, and substance abuse.

- **Stress Management Workshops**: Workshops that teach techniques for managing stress effectively.

- **Wellness Resources**: Access to fitness programs, nutritional advice, and other health-related information.

- **Financial Counseling**: Assistance with managing personal finances, debt, and budgeting.

- **Legal Assistance**: Help with legal issues, including wills, contracts, and other legal matters.

Case Study: A Multinational Company's EAP Success

Consider the example of a multinational company that implemented an EAP to address increasing stress levels among its employees. By offering a comprehensive EAP that included counseling, stress management workshops, and wellness resources, the company saw a significant decrease in employee absenteeism and an increase in overall job satisfaction. Employees reported feeling more supported and better equipped to handle their work and personal challenges.

Confidentiality

Understanding Privacy Protections

One of the primary concerns employees have when using EAP services is confidentiality. It's important to know that EAP services are confidential and separate from the organization's management structure. This means:

- **Private Sessions**: Sessions with counselors or other EAP providers are private and confidential.

- **No Reporting to Management**: Information shared with EAP counselors is not reported back to management without the employee's consent.

- **Anonymous Access**: Many EAPs offer anonymous access to online resources and hotlines.

Real-World Example

In a healthcare organization, employees were initially hesitant to use the EAP services due to concerns about

privacy. After the company conducted informational sessions emphasizing the confidentiality of the EAP, usage of the program increased significantly. Employees felt reassured that they could seek help without fear of repercussions.

Take Advantage of Counseling

Free or Subsidized Counseling Sessions

Many EAPs provide free or subsidized counseling sessions. These sessions can be invaluable for addressing stressors and mental health issues. Here's how to make the most of this benefit:

- **Identify Your Needs**: Determine what issues you want to address, such as stress, anxiety, or work-life balance.

- **Schedule Regular Sessions**: Regular counseling sessions can provide ongoing support and help you develop coping strategies.

- **Follow Professional Advice**: Be open to the advice and techniques provided by your counselor.

Illustration: Personal Transformation Through EAP Counseling

An employee at a large tech company was experiencing severe burnout due to a demanding work schedule. After using the EAP to access counseling services, the employee learned effective stress management techniques and received guidance on setting healthier work boundaries. As a result, their mental health improved, and they became more productive at work.

Educational Workshops

Attending Workshops and Training Sessions

EAPs often offer workshops and training sessions on various topics related to mental health and well-being.

These can provide valuable tools and techniques for managing stress and improving work-life balance.

Topics Covered

- **Stress Management**: Techniques for reducing and managing stress, such as mindfulness and relaxation exercises.

- **Time Management**: Strategies for organizing your time effectively to balance work and personal life.

- **Healthy Living**: Information on nutrition, exercise, and maintaining a healthy lifestyle.

Example: Effective Use of Workshops

At a financial services firm, employees were invited to attend a series of stress management workshops offered through their EAP. These workshops included sessions on mindfulness meditation, time management, and healthy living. Participants reported feeling more equipped to handle work pressures and noticed a significant reduction in their stress levels.

Strengthening Personal Relationships

Your personal relationships can be a source of immense support and comfort. Strengthening these bonds is essential for your overall well-being and can play a crucial role in overcoming burnout. Here's how to build and maintain a strong network of personal relationships:

Building a Network of Support

Identify Key Supporters

Recognize who in your life is supportive and understanding. This could include family members, friends, or colleagues.

- **Family Members**: Immediate and extended family can provide emotional support and practical assistance.

- **Friends**: Close friends can offer a listening ear and companionship.

- **Colleagues**: Trusted colleagues can provide professional support and share strategies for managing work-related stress.

Illustration: A Support Network in Action

Consider Jane, a marketing executive who was feeling overwhelmed by her workload. She identified her spouse, a close friend, and a trusted colleague as her key supporters. By regularly communicating with them and sharing her struggles, she received emotional support, practical advice, and encouragement that helped her navigate her challenges.

Communicate Regularly

Regular communication strengthens bonds and ensures you have a support system in place. Make an effort to keep in touch with your support network.

- **Regular Check-Ins**: Schedule regular phone calls or meetups to stay connected.

- **Share Your Experiences**: Be open about your struggles and successes. Sharing your experiences can provide emotional relief and allow others to offer support and advice.

Example: Regular Communication for Stronger Bonds

John, a software developer, made it a point to have weekly coffee meetings with a group of close friends. These regular check-ins provided a platform to discuss work-related stress and share coping strategies. The mutual support and encouragement from these friends helped John maintain a positive outlook and better manage his stress.

Mutual Support

Support should be a two-way street. Be there for others when they need help. This mutual support can strengthen your relationships and create a more robust network.

- **Offer Help**: Be proactive in offering support to your friends and family when they need it.

- **Be a Good Listener**: Sometimes, providing support means simply listening and being present.

Example: Mutual Support in Practice

Sarah, a teacher, found that supporting her friend Lisa during a difficult time not only strengthened their bond but also gave her a sense of purpose and fulfillment. By being there for each other, both Sarah and Lisa were able to navigate their challenges more effectively.

Balancing Family and Friends

Balancing relationships with family and friends is crucial for maintaining a healthy personal life. Here are some strategies to help you achieve this balance:

Prioritize Quality Time

Make time for meaningful interactions with family and friends. This can be through regular get-togethers, phone calls, or even virtual meetings.

- **Regular Get-Togethers**: Schedule regular family dinners or outings with friends.

- **Phone Calls and Virtual Meetings**: Use technology to stay connected with loved ones who live far away.

Example: Quality Time with Family

David, a busy executive, made it a priority to have a weekly game night with his family. This regular activity provided a much-needed break from work stress and strengthened his bond with his children.

Set Boundaries

Establish boundaries to ensure that work doesn't encroach on your personal time. Let your loved ones know when you are available and when you need time for yourself.

- **Communicate Your Availability**: Clearly communicate your work hours and personal time to your family and friends.

- **Protect Personal Time**: Make sure to protect your personal time by not allowing work to intrude.

Example: Setting Boundaries

Maria, a project manager, set a rule that she would not check work emails after 7 PM. This boundary allowed her to spend uninterrupted quality time with her family in the evenings.

Plan Activities Together

Engage in activities that everyone enjoys. This can strengthen your bonds and provide a much-needed break from work stress.

- **Shared Hobbies**: Find hobbies that you and your loved ones enjoy and make time to do them together.

- **Special Outings**: Plan special outings or vacations to create lasting memories.

Example: Family Activities

The Smith family made it a tradition to go hiking together every weekend. This shared activity not only provided physical exercise but also offered an opportunity to bond and enjoy nature together.

Express Appreciation

Regularly show appreciation for the support your family and friends provide. This can be through simple gestures like thank you notes or more significant actions like planning a special outing.

- **Thank You Notes**: Write thank you notes to express your gratitude.

- **Special Outings**: Plan special outings or activities to show your appreciation.

Example: Expressing Appreciation

Lisa, a nurse, wrote personalized thank you notes to her family and friends who supported her during a challenging time at work. These notes not only expressed her gratitude but also strengthened her relationships.

Seeking Professional Help

Sometimes, professional help is necessary to overcome burnout and achieve work-life balance. Knowing when and how to seek this help is crucial for your well-being.

When and How to Find a Therapist

Recognize the Signs

It's important to recognize when you might need professional help. Signs that you may benefit from seeing a therapist include:

- **Persistent Stress**: Constant feeling of stress that doesn't go away with usual coping mechanisms.

- **Anxiety and Depression**: Symptoms of anxiety or depression that interfere with daily life.

- **Burnout**: Feeling completely overwhelmed and unable to cope with work or personal responsibilities.

How to Find a Therapist

Finding the right therapist can be a critical step in your journey to recovery.

- **Research**: Look for licensed therapists in your area. Online directories and referrals from friends or family can be helpful.

- **Initial Consultation**: Many therapists offer a free initial consultation. Use this opportunity to determine if their approach aligns with your needs.

- **Evaluate Fit**: It's important to find a therapist you feel comfortable with. Don't hesitate to try a few before making a decision.

Example: Finding the Right Therapist

John, an engineer, recognized that his persistent anxiety was affecting his work performance and personal life. He used an online directory to find a licensed therapist and scheduled an initial consultation. After a few sessions, he found a therapist whose approach and personality matched his needs, leading to significant improvements in his mental health.

Benefits of Coaching and Counseling

Understanding the Benefits

Both coaching and counseling offer unique benefits in addressing burnout and achieving work-life balance.

- **Counseling**: Focuses on understanding and addressing psychological issues. It can help you process emotions, develop coping strategies, and improve mental health.

- **Coaching**: Focuses on setting and achieving personal and professional goals. It can help you develop skills, improve performance, and create actionable plans.

Case Study: The Impact of Coaching

Sarah, a marketing manager, was struggling with work-life balance and career direction. She decided to work with a coach who helped her identify her career goals and develop a plan to achieve them. Through regular coaching sessions, Sarah learned time management techniques, improved her work performance, and found a better balance between her professional and personal life.

Combining Both Approaches

Many people find that combining counseling and coaching provides the best results. Counseling can help address underlying psychological issues, while coaching can provide practical strategies for achieving work-life balance.

Example: A Holistic Approach

Maria, a lawyer, sought both counseling and coaching to manage her burnout. Counseling helped her address the anxiety and stress she was experiencing, while coaching provided her with tools and strategies to better manage her workload and set boundaries. This combined approach led to significant improvements in her overall well-being and work performance.

Conclusion

Utilizing Employee Assistance Programs, strengthening personal relationships, and seeking professional help are all critical components in managing burnout and achieving work-life balance. By taking advantage of the resources available through EAPs, building a strong network of support, and knowing when to seek professional help, you can effectively navigate the challenges of burnout and improve your overall well-being. Remember, the journey to achieving work-life balance is ongoing, and regularly revisiting and adjusting your strategies is key to maintaining a healthy and fulfilling life.

Chapter Five

Creating a Balanced Work Environment

Creating a balanced work environment is essential for preventing burnout and promoting long-term well-being. This chapter will guide you on redesigning your workday, promoting a healthy workplace culture, and setting boundaries.

Redesigning Your Workday

A well-structured workday can significantly reduce stress and improve productivity.

Flexible Work Arrangements

In today's fast-paced world, the traditional 9-to-5 workday is no longer the only option for professionals. Flexible work arrangements have emerged as a powerful tool to help individuals balance their work and personal lives more effectively. These arrangements not only accommodate personal responsibilities but also enhance productivity and job satisfaction. Below is an in-depth exploration of various flexible work arrangements and their benefits.

Remote Work

The Rise of Remote Work

Remote work, also known as telecommuting, has gained immense popularity in recent years, particularly with the advent of technology that allows seamless communication and collaboration from anywhere in the world. The COVID-19 pandemic further accelerated this trend, with many companies realizing that employees can be just as productive, if not more so, when working from home.

Benefits of Remote Work

- **Reduced Commute Stress**: One of the most significant advantages of remote work is the elimination of the daily commute. Commuting can be a major source of stress, leading to physical and mental exhaustion even before the workday begins By working from home, employees can reclaim the time spent commuting and use it for more productive or restorative activities, such as exercise, family time, or hobbies.

- **Comfortable Working Environment**: Working from home allows employees to create a comfortable and personalized work environment. This could mean working from a cozy home office, sitting in a comfortable chair, or even working in a favorite café. A comfortable environment can significantly enhance focus and productivity.

- **Improved Work-Life Balance**: Remote work offers the flexibility to integrate work with personal life more seamlessly. For example, parents can manage their children's schedules more effectively, or individuals can attend to personal errands without disrupting their workday.

Example: A Successful Remote Work Arrangement

Consider Sarah, a graphic designer who negotiated a remote work arrangement with her employer. By eliminating her daily two-hour commute, Sarah was able to start her workday feeling more refreshed and focused. She also found that working in her personalized home office, surrounded by her favorite artwork and plants, boosted her creativity. As a result, her productivity increased, and she was able to meet project deadlines more efficiently.

Challenges and Solutions

While remote work offers numerous benefits, it also presents challenges, such as feelings of isolation and difficulty in separating work from personal life. To mitigate these challenges:

- **Regular Check-Ins**: Schedule regular virtual check-ins with your team to maintain a sense of connection and collaboration.

- **Set Boundaries**: Establish clear boundaries between work and personal time to avoid burnout. For example, designate a specific workspace in your home and adhere to a regular work schedule.

Flexible Hours

The Flexibility of Working Hours

Flexible working hours, or flex-time, allow employees to choose their working hours within a set range, as long as they meet their required number of hours each week. This flexibility enables individuals to work during their most productive times and better accommodate personal responsibilities.

Benefits of Flexible Hours

- **Enhanced Productivity**: People have different peak productivity times. Some are more productive in the early morning, while others may perform better in the afternoon or evening. Flexible hours allow employees to work during their peak times, leading to higher efficiency and better quality of work.

- **Better Personal Time Management**: Flexible hours provide the freedom to manage personal tasks, such as attending a child's school event, scheduling a medical appointment, or running errands, without the stress of conflicting work schedules.

Example: Flexible Hours in Practice

John, a software developer, negotiated flexible working hours with his employer. He chose to start his workday early in the morning, allowing him to finish by mid-afternoon. This schedule enabled John to pick up his children from school and spend quality time with them in the evening. He found that working during his peak productivity hours not only improved his work output but also reduced his stress levels.

Challenges and Solutions

Flex-time can be challenging in roles that require constant collaboration with team members who may have different working hours. To address this:

- **Core Hours**: Implement core hours where all team members are available for meetings and collaboration, ensuring that communication and teamwork are not compromised.

- **Clear Communication**: Use shared calendars and communication tools to keep everyone informed of each other's schedules and availability.

Compressed Workweeks

The Concept of Compressed Workweeks

A compressed workweek allows employees to work the equivalent of a full-time schedule in fewer days. For example, instead of working five 8-hour days, an employee might work four 10-hour days. This arrangement provides extended time off, which can be used to recharge, pursue personal interests, or spend time with family.

Benefits of Compressed Workweeks

- **Extended Time Off**: A compressed workweek provides employees with an extra day off each week, which can be used for rest, leisure activities, or personal responsibilities. This extra day off can help reduce stress and prevent burnout.

- **Increased Focus**: Working longer hours on fewer days can help employees focus on completing tasks without the need for frequent interruptions. This can lead to higher productivity during work hours.

Example: The Benefits of a Compressed Workweek

Emily, a project manager at a marketing agency, negotiated a compressed workweek, working four 10-

hour days instead of the traditional five 8-hour days. This arrangement allowed her to take Fridays off, which she used to volunteer at a local charity. The extra day off helped Emily maintain a healthy work-life balance and prevented burnout, while her productivity during the workweek remained high.

Challenges and Solutions

Compressed workweeks can lead to longer workdays, which may be tiring for some employees. To address this:

- **Regular Breaks**: Encourage taking short breaks throughout the day to maintain energy levels and prevent fatigue.

- **Efficient Time Management**: Prioritize tasks and manage time effectively to ensure that the longer workdays are productive and not overwhelming.

Job Sharing

The Job Sharing Model

Job sharing is a flexible work arrangement where two employees share the responsibilities of one full-time job. This arrangement allows both individuals to work part-time while ensuring that the job's responsibilities are fully covered. Job sharing can be particularly beneficial for employees seeking more personal time without sacrificing their careers.

Benefits of Job Sharing

- **Reduced Workload**: Job sharing reduces the workload for each employee, providing more time for personal responsibilities and reducing the risk of burnout.

- **Maintained Career Progression**: By sharing a full-time role, both employees can maintain their career trajectory while enjoying the benefits of part-time work.

Example: Successful Job Sharing

Lisa and Mark, both experienced HR professionals, decided to enter a job-sharing arrangement. By splitting the responsibilities of the HR manager role, they each worked three days a week. This arrangement allowed Lisa to spend more time with her young children and Mark to pursue further education. The company benefited from having two experienced professionals sharing their expertise, and both employees felt more balanced and fulfilled.

Challenges and Solutions

Job sharing requires excellent communication and coordination between the two employees sharing the role. To ensure success:

- **Clear Division of Responsibilities**: Clearly define and document the responsibilities and tasks for each employee to avoid overlap or gaps.

- **Regular Communication**: Schedule regular meetings between the job sharers to discuss progress, challenges, and any necessary handovers.

Creating a Productive Workspace

A productive workspace is essential for maintaining focus, reducing stress, and enhancing overall work performance. Whether working from home or in an office, the environment in which you work plays a crucial role in your productivity and well-being.

Ergonomic Setup

Importance of Ergonomics

An ergonomically designed workspace is crucial for preventing physical strain and promoting long-term health. Ergonomics refers to designing a workspace that fits the user's needs, minimizing discomfort and the risk of injury.

Key Elements of an Ergonomic Workspace

- **Chair**: Invest in a chair that supports your lower back and encourages good posture. Adjustable chairs with lumbar support are ideal for maintaining comfort during long hours of work.

- **Desk**: Ensure that your desk is at the correct height to prevent strain on your wrists and shoulders. Your elbows should be at a 90-degree angle when typing, and your feet should rest flat on the floor.

- **Monitor Position**: Position your computer monitor at eye level and about an arm's length away from you. This reduces strain on your neck and eyes.

Example: Ergonomics in Practice

David, an accountant, experienced chronic back pain due to poor posture at his desk. After investing in an ergonomic chair and adjusting his desk setup, he noticed a significant reduction in pain and an improvement in his overall comfort while working. This ergonomic setup also helped David focus better, as he was no longer distracted by physical discomfort.

Additional Tips

- **Keyboard and Mouse**: Use a keyboard and mouse that are comfortable and positioned to reduce strain on your hands and wrists. Consider using ergonomic accessories if necessary.

- **Regular Movement**: Even with an ergonomic setup, it's important to take regular breaks to move around and stretch. This helps prevent stiffness and promotes circulation.

Minimize Distractions

Identifying and Reducing Distractions

Distractions can significantly impact productivity, especially when working in a non-traditional workspace such as home. Identifying and minimizing these distractions is key to maintaining focus.

Common Distractions and Solutions

- **Noise**: Noise from household activities, neighbors, or street traffic can be distracting. Consider using noise-canceling headphones or white noise machines to block out unwanted sounds.

- **Clutter**: A cluttered workspace can be visually distracting and increase stress. Keep your workspace organized and free of unnecessary items.

- **Family Members or Roommates**: If you live with others, it's important to set boundaries. Let them know your work hours and ask for quiet time during those periods.

Example: Minimizing Distractions

Anna, a freelance writer, found it challenging to concentrate with the noise of her busy household. She invested in a pair of noise-canceling headphones and designated a quiet room as her workspace. By minimizing distractions, Anna was able to write more efficiently and meet her deadlines without feeling overwhelmed.

Personalize Your Space

The Power of Personalization

Personalizing your workspace can make it more inviting and enjoyable, leading to increased motivation and satisfaction. A workspace that reflects your personality and preferences can boost your mood and make the workday more pleasant.

Ways to Personalize Your Workspace

- **Decor**: Add personal touches like family photos, artwork, or motivational quotes. These items can serve as reminders of what matters most to you and provide inspiration throughout the day.

- **Plants**: Incorporating plants into your workspace can improve air quality and create a calming atmosphere. Studies have shown that having plants in the workplace can reduce stress and increase productivity.

- **Comfort Items**: Include items that make you feel comfortable, such as a cozy blanket, a favorite mug, or a scented candle. These small comforts can make a big difference in your work environment.

Example: Personalizing Your Workspace

Megan, a customer service representative, personalized her workspace by adding photos of her family, a small plant on her desk, and a colorful calendar. These personal touches made her feel more connected to her work and improved her overall mood during the workday.

Organization

The Importance of Organization

An organized workspace is essential for reducing stress and increasing productivity. A clutter-free environment allows you to focus on your tasks without the distraction of searching for misplaced items or dealing with unnecessary clutter.

Tips for Organizing Your Workspace

- **De-cluster Regularly**: Regularly de-cluster your workspace by removing items you no longer need. This can include old paperwork, unused office supplies, or outdated equipment.

- **Storage Solutions**: Invest in storage solutions such as filing cabinets, shelves, or drawer organizers. These can help keep your workspace tidy and ensure that everything has its place.

- **Digital Organization**: Keep your digital workspace organized as well. Regularly clean up your desktop, organize files into folders, and back up important data.

Example: The Impact of Organization

Tom, a sales manager, found that his cluttered desk was negatively impacting his productivity. After organizing his workspace and implementing a filing system, Tom noticed that he was able to find documents more quickly and felt less overwhelmed by his workload.

Promoting a Healthy Workplace Culture

A healthy workplace culture is essential for employee well-being, engagement, and productivity. It encompasses the values, behaviors, and practices that define the work environment and influence how employees interact with one another and approach their work.

The Role of Leadership

Leadership's Influence on Workplace Culture

Leadership plays a pivotal role in shaping and maintaining a healthy workplace culture. Leaders set the tone for the organization by modeling positive behaviors, setting clear expectations, and fostering an inclusive and supportive environment.

Strategies for Promoting a Healthy Culture

- **Open Communication**: Encourage open and transparent communication between employees and management. This can be achieved through regular team meetings, feedback sessions, and an open-door policy.

- **Employee Recognition**: Recognize and reward employees for their contributions and achievements.

- This can include formal recognition programs, bonuses, or simple acknowledgments during meetings.

- **Work-Life Balance**: Promote a culture that values work-life balance by encouraging employees to take breaks, use their vacation days, and set boundaries between work and personal life.

Example: Leadership's Role in Culture

At a mid-sized tech company, the CEO made it a priority to promote a healthy workplace culture by regularly communicating with employees, recognizing their achievements, and encouraging work-life balance. This approach led to higher employee satisfaction, lower turnover rates, and increased productivity across the company.

Encouraging Collaboration and Teamwork

The Importance of Collaboration

Collaboration and teamwork are essential components of a healthy workplace culture. When employees work together effectively, they can achieve better results, foster innovation, and build stronger relationships.

Strategies for Encouraging Collaboration

- **Team Building Activities**: Organize team-building activities that encourage collaboration and help employees build trust and rapport with one another.

- **Cross-Functional Teams**: Encourage collaboration between different departments or teams within the organization. This can lead to new ideas and improved problem-solving.

- **Collaborative Tools**: Provide employees with tools and technologies that facilitate collaboration, such as project management software, communication platforms, and shared workspaces.

Example: Successful Collaboration

A marketing agency implemented regular team-building activities and invested in collaborative tools to improve teamwork. As a result, employees felt more connected, and the quality of their work improved, leading to better client outcomes and higher employee morale.

Supporting Employee Well-Being

The Importance of Well-Being

Employee well-being is a critical component of a healthy workplace culture. When employees feel supported and valued, they are more likely to be engaged, motivated, and productive.

Strategies for Supporting Well-Being

- **Wellness Programs**: Implement wellness programs that promote physical and mental health, such as fitness challenges, stress management workshops, and access to counseling services.

- **Workplace Flexibility**: Offer flexible work arrangements, as discussed earlier, to help employees balance their work and personal lives.

- **Mental Health Support**: Provide resources and support for mental health, including access to Employee Assistance Programs (EAPs) and promoting a stigma-free environment.

Example: A Focus on Well-Being

A financial services firm introduced a comprehensive wellness program that included fitness classes, mental health workshops, and flexible working hours. This focus on employee well-being led to a noticeable improvement in employee satisfaction, reduced absenteeism, and increased productivity.

Key Point

Flexible work arrangements, a productive workspace, and a healthy workplace culture are all critical components in achieving work-life balance and preventing burnout.

By negotiating flexible work options, creating a comfortable and organized workspace, and promoting a supportive work environment, individuals can improve their well-being and enhance their productivity. As the workplace continues to evolve, these strategies will remain essential for fostering a balanced and fulfilling professional life.

Encouraging Open Communication

Open communication fosters trust and transparency within the workplace.

- **Regular Check-Ins:** Schedule regular one-on-one check-ins with your team members or manager. Use these sessions to discuss progress, address concerns, and provide feedback.

- **Team Meetings:** Hold regular team meetings to ensure everyone is aligned and has a platform to voice their opinions. Encourage open and respectful communication.

- **Anonymous Feedback:** Provide options for anonymous feedback. This allows employees to share their thoughts and concerns without fear of retribution.

- **Active Listening:** Practice active listening by fully engaging in conversations, showing empathy, and providing thoughtful responses.

Implementing Wellness Programs

Wellness programs can significantly enhance employee well-being and reduce burnout.

- **Health and Fitness Programs:** Offer health and fitness programs, such as gym memberships, yoga classes, or wellness challenges. Encourage participation through incentives and regular updates.

- **Mental Health Support:** Provide resources for mental health support, including access to counselors, stress management workshops, and mental health days.

- **Work-Life Balance Initiatives:** Implement initiatives that promote work-life balance, such as flexible work hours, remote work options, and family-friendly policies.

- **Recognition and Rewards:** Recognize and reward employees for their contributions. This can boost morale and create a positive work environment.

Setting Boundaries

Setting clear boundaries is essential for maintaining a healthy work-life balance.

Work Hours and Availability

Establishing boundaries around work hours and availability can prevent burnout.

- **Set Work Hours:** Define your work hours and stick to them. Communicate these hours to your colleagues and managers to manage expectations.

- **Turn Off Notifications:** Turn off work notifications outside of your defined work hours. This helps you disconnect and recharge.

- **Respect Others' Boundaries:** Respect the work hours and boundaries of your colleagues. Avoid contacting them outside of their working hours unless it's an emergency.

- **Time Blocking:** Use time blocking to schedule dedicated work periods and breaks. This can improve focus and prevent burnout.

Managing Work-Related Stress

Effective stress management strategies are crucial for maintaining a balanced work environment.

- **Stress Management Techniques:** Practice stress management techniques such as deep breathing, mindfulness, and exercise. Incorporate these practices into your daily routine.

- **Workload Management:** Regularly review and adjust your workload to ensure it's manageable. Delegate tasks where possible and communicate with your manager if you're feeling overwhelmed.

- **Take Breaks:** Schedule regular breaks throughout your workday. Use this time to stretch, walk, or engage in a relaxing activity.

- **Seek Support:** If work-related stress becomes overwhelming, seek support from your manager, colleagues, or a professional counselor.

Chapter Six

Enhancing Personal Well-Being

Achieving a balanced life requires more than just managing work-related stress; it also involves enhancing your personal well-being. This chapter will explore techniques for developing mindfulness and resilience, the importance of pursuing hobbies and interests, and maintaining a healthy lifestyle.

Developing Mindfulness and Resilience

Mindfulness and resilience are essential tools for managing stress and maintaining overall well-being.

Techniques for Mindfulness

Mindfulness involves being fully present in the moment and aware of your thoughts, feelings, and surroundings without judgment. Here are some techniques to develop mindfulness:

- **Mindful Breathing:** Focus on your breath as you inhale and exhale. Notice the sensation of the air entering and leaving your body. If your mind wanders, gently bring your attention back to your breath. This practice can be done anywhere, at any time, and helps to calm the mind and reduce stress.

- **Body Scan Meditation:** Lie down or sit comfortably. Close your eyes and slowly bring your attention to different parts of your body, starting from your toes and moving up to your head. Notice any sensations, tension, or discomfort. This practice promotes relaxation and body awareness.

- **Mindful Walking:** During a walk, focus on the sensation of your feet touching the ground, the movement of your body, and the sights and sounds around you. This practice helps you connect with the present moment and can be particularly refreshing if done outdoors.

- **Mindful Eating:** Pay full attention to the taste, texture, and smell of your food. Eat slowly and savor each bite.

This practice can enhance your appreciation of food and improve your eating habits.

Building Emotional Resilience

Emotional resilience is the capacity to navigate through life's challenges with strength, adaptability, and a sense of purpose. It is the inner strength that enables you to recover from setbacks, manage stress, and continue forward with a positive outlook. Building emotional resilience is crucial for maintaining mental well-being and thriving in both personal and professional life. Below are strategies to help you develop and enhance your emotional resilience.

Positive Thinking

The Power of a Positive Outlook

Positive thinking is a cornerstone of emotional resilience. It involves maintaining a hopeful and optimistic perspective, even in the face of adversity. A positive outlook does not mean ignoring difficulties but rather approaching challenges with a belief in your ability to overcome them. Research has shown that individuals who cultivate a positive mindset are more likely to experience better mental and physical health outcomes, including lower levels of stress and depression.

Strategies to Cultivate Positive Thinking

- **Focus on Strengths**: Regularly remind yourself of your strengths and past achievements. This can boost your confidence and reinforce your belief in your ability to handle future challenges. For example, if you have successfully managed a demanding project in the past, recalling that experience can provide reassurance during a current stressful situation.

- **Practice Gratitude**: Gratitude is a powerful tool for shifting your mindset towards positivity. By regularly acknowledging and appreciating the positive aspects of your life, you can create a more optimistic outlook. Consider keeping a gratitude journal where you write down three things you are thankful for each day. Over time, this practice can help you become more attuned to the positive aspects of your life, even when faced with difficulties.

Example: The Impact of Positive Thinking

Jane, a teacher facing the pressures of balancing work and family life, found herself overwhelmed by stress. She began practicing gratitude by writing down three things she appreciated each day, such as the support of her colleagues or the small achievements of her students. Over time, Jane noticed a significant improvement in her mood and ability to cope with the daily stresses of her job. Her positive outlook also had a ripple effect, enhancing her interactions with students and colleagues.

Develop Coping Strategies

The Importance of Coping Mechanisms

Coping strategies are essential tools for managing stress and building emotional resilience. These strategies help you navigate through challenging situations, providing immediate relief and long-term support. Everyone's coping mechanisms are different, so it's important to identify what works best for you.

Common Coping Strategies

- **Deep Breathing**: Deep breathing is a simple yet effective technique for managing stress in the moment. By focusing on slow, controlled breaths, you can activate the body's relaxation response, reducing feelings of anxiety and tension. For instance, when faced with a stressful situation, taking a few deep breaths can help calm your mind and body, allowing you to respond more thoughtfully rather than react impulsively.

- **Journaling**: Writing down your thoughts and feelings can be a powerful way to process emotions and gain clarity. Journaling allows you to reflect on your experiences, identify patterns, and release pent-up emotions. For example, after a particularly challenging day, spending a few minutes journaling about your thoughts and feelings can provide a sense of relief and help you gain a new perspective on the situation.

- **Talking to a Friend**: Social support is a crucial element of emotional resilience. Talking to a trusted friend or family member about your stressors can provide emotional relief and offer new insights or solutions.

- Sharing your experiences with someone who understands and empathizes can also help you feel less alone in your struggles.

Example: Coping Strategies in Action

Mark, a marketing executive, often felt overwhelmed by the demands of his job. He found that deep breathing exercises helped him manage stress during high-pressure meetings. Additionally, he began journaling in the evenings, which allowed him to reflect on his day and clear his mind before going to bed. By incorporating these coping strategies into his routine, Mark was better equipped to handle the challenges of his role and maintain a sense of balance.

Seek Support

The Role of Social Support in Resilience

Building strong relationships with family, friends, and colleagues is essential for emotional resilience. A supportive network provides emotional comfort, practical assistance, and a sense of belonging during difficult times. Research has shown that individuals with strong social connections are more resilient and better able to cope with stress.

Strategies for Building and Maintaining Support Networks

- **Identify Your Support System**: Recognize the people in your life who provide emotional support and understanding. This could include family members, close friends, colleagues, or even support groups. Knowing who you can turn to during challenging times is crucial for building resilience.

- **Communicate Openly**: Regular communication with your support network is key to maintaining strong relationships. Share your experiences, thoughts, and feelings with those you trust. Open communication fosters deeper connections and ensures that you have a reliable support system when needed.

- **Don't Hesitate to Reach Out**: It's important to seek help when you need it. Whether it's asking for advice, emotional support, or practical assistance, reaching out to your support network can provide relief and help you navigate through difficult situations. Remember, seeking help is a sign of strength, not weakness.

Example: The Importance of Support

Emma, a small business owner, experienced significant stress when her business faced financial difficulties. She reached out to her close friends and family for emotional support and practical advice. Their encouragement and assistance helped Emma stay motivated and focused on finding solutions. By leaning on her support network, Emma was able to navigate the challenges and eventually turn her business around.

Learn from Experience

The Value of Reflection

Learning from past experiences is a powerful way to build emotional resilience. Reflecting on how you have overcome previous challenges can boost your confidence and prepare you for future stressors. Each experience, whether positive or negative, offers valuable lessons that can inform your approach to new situations.

Strategies for Learning from Experience

- **Reflect on Past Challenges**: Take time to think about the difficulties you have faced in the past and how you managed to overcome them. Consider what strategies worked well and what you might do differently in the future. This reflection can reinforce your belief in your ability to handle future challenges.

- **Document Your Journey**: Keeping a record of your experiences, such as through journaling or creating a personal success log, can help you track your growth and resilience over time. Reviewing these records can provide motivation and remind you of your strengths during tough times.

- **Apply Lessons Learned**: Use the insights gained from past experiences to inform your approach to current and future challenges. For example, if you successfully managed stress during a previous project by practicing time management, apply those same techniques to new projects.

Example: Learning from Experience

Sophie, a nurse, faced a particularly difficult period during the height of the COVID-19 pandemic. Reflecting on her past experiences of handling stressful situations in the healthcare setting, she realized that maintaining a structured routine and seeking support from colleagues had been key to her resilience. By applying these lessons during the pandemic, Sophie was able to manage her stress more effectively and provide quality care to her patients.

Scenario: Imagine Sarah, a marketing manager, who often feels overwhelmed by her workload. She decides to practice mindfulness by dedicating 10 minutes each morning to mindful breathing. Over time, Sarah notices she feels more focused and less stressed throughout the day. She also starts journaling to reflect on her daily experiences, which helps her gain perspective and build resilience.

Key Point

Building emotional resilience is an ongoing process that involves cultivating a positive mindset, developing effective coping strategies, seeking support, and learning from past experiences. By implementing these strategies, you can enhance your ability to adapt to stressful situations, recover from setbacks, and maintain a sense of balance and well-being. Emotional resilience is not just about surviving challenges—it's about thriving in the face of adversity and emerging stronger on the other side.

Pursuing Hobbies and Interests

Engaging in hobbies and personal interests is crucial for relaxation and mental well-being.

Finding Time for Personal Passions

Making time for hobbies and interests can be challenging, but it's essential for a balanced life.

- **Schedule It:** Treat hobbies like any other important appointment. Schedule dedicated time in your calendar for activities you enjoy.

- **Start Small:** Begin with short periods dedicated to your hobby. Even 15-30 minutes a day can make a difference.

- **Combine Activities:** If time is limited, combine hobbies with other activities.

- For example, listen to an audiobook while exercising or sketch while watching TV.

- **Set Realistic Goals:** Avoid setting overly ambitious goals that may lead to frustration. Focus on enjoying the process rather than achieving perfection.

Benefits of Creative Outlets

Creative outlets offer numerous benefits for mental health and well-being.

- **Stress Relief:** Engaging in creative activities such as painting, writing, or playing music can provide an escape from daily stressors and promote relaxation.

- **Self-Expression:** Creative outlets allow you to express emotions and thoughts that may be difficult to articulate otherwise. This can be therapeutic and enhance emotional well-being.

- **Cognitive Benefits:** Activities like playing a musical instrument or crafting can improve cognitive functions such as concentration, problem-solving, and memory.

- **Social Connection:** Joining groups or clubs related to your interests can provide opportunities to meet like-minded individuals and build a supportive community.

Scenario: John, a software developer, enjoys playing the guitar but often finds it hard to make time for his hobby. He decides to schedule 20 minutes of guitar practice every evening before dinner. This routine not only helps him relax after a long day but also improves his mood and overall sense of well-being.

Maintaining a Healthy Lifestyle

A healthy lifestyle is the foundation of personal well-being. This includes regular exercise, proper nutrition, and adequate hydration.

Exercise Routines

Regular physical activity is essential for maintaining physical and mental health.

- **Consistency:** Aim for at least 150 minutes of moderate aerobic activity or 75 minutes of vigorous activity per week, along with muscle-strengthening exercises on two or more days a week.

- **Enjoyment:** Choose activities you enjoy to make exercise a regular part of your routine. This could include walking, running, cycling, swimming, yoga, or team sports.

- **Variety:** Mix different types of exercises to keep your routine interesting and work different muscle groups. This can include cardio, strength training, flexibility exercises, and balance exercises.

- **Social Engagement:** Exercise with friends or join a fitness class. Social interactions can make workouts more enjoyable and provide motivation.

Nutritional Choices and Hydration

A balanced diet and proper hydration are crucial for overall health.

- **Balanced Diet:** Focus on a diet rich in fruits, vegetables, whole grains, lean proteins, and healthy fats. Limit processed foods, sugar, and excessive salt.

- **Mindful Eating:** Practice mindful eating by paying attention to hunger and fullness cues. Avoid distractions while eating and savor each bite.

- **Hydration:** Drink plenty of water throughout the day. The general recommendation is about eight 8-ounce glasses of water a day, but individual needs can vary.

- **Healthy Snacks:** Choose healthy snacks such as fruits, nuts, yogurt, or vegetable sticks. Avoid high-sugar and high-fat snacks that provide little nutritional value.

Scenario: Emily, a busy lawyer, struggles to find time for exercise and often skips meals or eats fast food. She decides to make small changes by incorporating a 30-minute morning walk into her routine and preparing healthy snacks like carrot sticks and hummus. Over time, Emily feels more energetic and focused, and her overall health improves.

Chapter Seven

Implementing Work-Life Balance Practices

Achieving a balanced life requires a strategic approach to managing both professional and personal responsibilities. This chapter will explore creating a work-life balance plan, aligning professional and personal goals, and dealing with setbacks.

Creating a Work-Life Balance Plan

A work-life balance plan provides a roadmap for managing your time and responsibilities effectively.

Setting Clear Boundaries

Establishing clear boundaries between work and personal life is a fundamental aspect of maintaining a healthy work-life balance. Boundaries serve as invisible lines that define the limits of our responsibilities, interactions, and time commitments. Without these boundaries, the lines between work and personal life can blur, leading to burnout, stress, and a lack of fulfillment in both areas. Here's an in-depth look at how you can set and maintain clear boundaries, supported by examples and practical strategies.

Define Work Hours

One of the most effective ways to establish a boundary between work and personal life is by setting specific work hours. This involves determining when your workday starts and ends and making a conscious effort to adhere to this schedule.

Communicating Work Hours

- **With Colleagues**: It's important to communicate your defined work hours to your colleagues and supervisors. By doing so, you set clear expectations about when you are available for work-related tasks and when you are not. For example, if your workday ends at 5:00 PM, let your colleagues know that you will not be responding to emails or taking work calls after that time.

- This not only helps you maintain a work-life balance but also encourages others to respect your time.

- **With Family Members**: If you work from home, it's equally important to communicate your work hours to your family members. This helps them understand when you are available for personal interactions and when you need to focus on work. For instance, you can let your family know that during your designated work hours, you should not be disturbed unless it's an emergency. This can prevent interruptions and help you stay productive during work hours.

Example: The Importance of Defined Work Hours

Sarah, a freelance graphic designer, struggled with maintaining boundaries between her work and personal life. She often found herself working late into the night, which affected her relationships and personal well-being. After realizing the impact of her lack of boundaries, Sarah decided to set specific work hours from 9:00 AM to 5:00 PM. She communicated these hours to her clients and family, making it clear that she would not be available outside these times. As a result, Sarah was able to reclaim her evenings for personal activities and experienced a significant improvement in her work-life balance.

Designate Workspaces

Creating a physical boundary between work and personal life is essential, especially for those who work from home. Designating a specific workspace can help you mentally separate work from personal activities, leading to increased focus and productivity during work hours and better relaxation during personal time.

Creating an Effective Workspace

- **Separate Spaces**: Whenever possible, choose a workspace that is separate from personal areas like the bedroom or living room. This separation creates a physical boundary that signals to your brain when it's time to work and when it's time to relax. For example, if you have a spare room, convert it into a home office where you can work without distractions. If space is limited, designate a corner of a room specifically for work, using a desk and office chair to create a professional environment.

- **Ergonomic Considerations**: Ensure that your workspace is ergonomically designed to support your health and well-being. This includes having a comfortable chair, a desk at the right height, and your computer screen positioned at eye level. A well-designed workspace can reduce physical strain and improve your focus during work hours.

Example: The Impact of Designated Workspaces

John, a software developer, initially worked from his dining table, which was also the center of family life. The constant interruptions from family members and the lack of a dedicated workspace made it difficult for him to concentrate. John decided to transform a small, unused area in his bedroom into a home office. He added a desk, chair, and some personal touches to make the space inviting. By creating a designated workspace, John was able to increase his productivity and clearly separate his work and personal life.

Turn Off Work Notifications

In today's digital age, work-related notifications can easily infiltrate our personal time, making it difficult to fully disconnect from work. Turning off work notifications outside of work hours is a crucial step in establishing boundaries and protecting your personal time.

Managing Work Notifications

- **Use Do Not Disturb Mode**: Most smartphones and computers have a "Do Not Disturb" mode that you can activate during non-work hours. This feature blocks notifications from emails, messaging apps, and other work-related platforms, allowing you to focus on personal activities without interruptions. For instance, you can set your devices to automatically enter "Do Not Disturb" mode at 6:00 PM, signaling the end of your workday.

- **Separate Work and Personal Devices**: If possible, use separate devices for work and personal activities. This allows you to turn off your work devices at the end of the workday while still being accessible to family and friends through your personal device. By keeping work and personal communications separate, you can better manage your boundaries.

Example: The Benefit of Turning Off Work Notifications

Emily, a marketing manager, used to keep her work email notifications on her phone active 24/7. This constant influx of emails made it difficult for her to relax during evenings and weekends. After attending a workshop on work-life balance, Emily decided to turn off her work notifications outside of her defined work hours. This simple change allowed her to enjoy her personal time without the stress of incoming work emails, leading to a more balanced and fulfilling life.

Learn to Say No

Learning to say no is a critical skill for maintaining boundaries and protecting your time and energy. Whether it's declining additional work assignments or personal commitments, saying no allows you to prioritize tasks that align with your goals and well-being.

Strategies for Saying No

- **Prioritize Your Commitments**: Before agreeing to take on additional tasks, evaluate whether they align with your current goals and responsibilities. If a new task doesn't contribute to your priorities or is likely to overwhelm you, it's okay to decline. For example, if you're asked to take on a new project at work but are already at capacity, explain your current workload to your supervisor and suggest revisiting the request at a later time.

- **Be Polite but Firm**: When saying no, it's important to be polite yet firm. You can decline additional responsibilities without feeling guilty by being honest about your limits. For instance, if a colleague asks you to help with a task outside your work hours, you can respond by saying, "I'm currently focusing on my existing projects and need to maintain my work-life balance. I'm unable to take on additional work at this time."

Example: The Power of Saying No

James, a senior accountant, often found himself overwhelmed with work because he had difficulty saying no to requests from colleagues and clients. As a result, he worked long hours and rarely had time for himself. After attending a time management seminar, James learned the importance of setting boundaries by saying no.

He began to evaluate new requests based on his current workload and priorities. By politely declining tasks that didn't align with his goals, James was able to reduce his workload, improve his work-life balance, and perform better in his core responsibilities.

Allocating Time for Personal Activities

Balancing work with personal activities is essential for maintaining a fulfilling and well-rounded life. By intentionally allocating time for personal activities, you can ensure that you have opportunities for relaxation, enjoyment, and self-care, which are crucial for preventing burnout and maintaining overall well-being.

Time Blocking

Time blocking is a time management technique that involves allocating specific blocks of time for different activities throughout the day. This method helps you organize your schedule, prioritize tasks, and ensure that both work and personal activities receive the attention they deserve.

Implementing Time Blocking

- **Create a Daily Schedule**: Start by creating a daily schedule that includes time blocks for work, family, hobbies, self-care, and other personal activities. For example, you might block off 9:00 AM to 12:00 PM for work tasks, 12:00 PM to 1:00 PM for lunch and relaxation, and 5:00 PM to 6:00 PM for exercise or a hobby. By structuring your day in this way, you can ensure that all aspects of your life receive adequate time and attention.

- **Stick to Your Schedule**: Once you've created your time blocks, commit to sticking to them as closely as possible. While flexibility is important, try to honor the time you've allocated for personal activities, just as you would for work-related tasks. This consistency helps reinforce the boundaries you've set and ensures that personal time is not neglected.

Example: Time Blocking for Balance

Laura, a busy lawyer, struggled to find time for herself amid her demanding work schedule. After learning about time blocking, she decided to create a daily schedule that included specific time blocks for work, exercise, and spending time with her family. By following this schedule, Laura was able to maintain her professional responsibilities while also prioritizing her well-being and personal relationships.

Prioritize Self-Care

Self-care is a vital component of a balanced life. By prioritizing self-care activities, you can recharge your energy, reduce stress, and improve your overall quality of life.

Incorporating Self-Care into Your Routine

- **Make It Non-Negotiable**: Treat self-care as a non-negotiable part of your daily routine. This could include activities such as exercise, meditation, reading, or taking a relaxing bath. For example, you might commit to a daily 30-minute walk after work to unwind and clear your mind. By making self-care a priority, you ensure that you are taking time to nurture your physical, mental, and emotional well-being.

- **Tailor Self-Care to Your Needs**: Self-care looks different for everyone, so it's important to choose activities that resonate with you and meet your needs. Whether it's engaging in creative hobbies, practicing mindfulness, or spending time in nature, find what works best for you and make it a regular part of your life.

Example: The Importance of Prioritizing Self-Care

Mia, a high school teacher, used to feel constantly drained by the demands of her job. She realized that she wasn't taking enough time for herself, which led to burnout. Mia decided to prioritize self-care by scheduling 20 minutes of meditation each morning and a weekly yoga class. These practices helped Mia manage her stress, feel more energized, and approach her work with renewed enthusiasm.

Flexible Scheduling

A flexible schedule allows you to adjust your work hours around personal commitments, providing greater autonomy over how you manage your time. This flexibility can lead to improved work-life balance and a better ability to meet both professional and personal needs.

Adopting a Flexible Schedule

- **Negotiate Flexibility with Your Employer**: If your job allows it, consider negotiating a flexible schedule with your employer. This could include options such as starting work earlier or later, working compressed workweeks, or occasionally working from home. For example, if you have personal commitments in the afternoon, you might arrange to start your workday earlier so you can finish by mid-afternoon.

- **Use Flexibility to Your Advantage**: Once you have a flexible schedule, use it to balance your work and personal responsibilities more effectively. For instance, if you know you're more productive in the mornings, you might choose to focus on complex tasks during that time and reserve the afternoons for personal activities or less demanding work.

Example: The Benefits of Flexible Scheduling

David, a project manager, found it challenging to balance his work responsibilities with his role as a father. After discussing his needs with his employer, David was able to adopt a flexible schedule that allowed him to work from 7:00 AM to 3:00 PM. This change gave David more time in the afternoons to spend with his children, attend their school events, and manage household responsibilities. The flexible schedule not only improved David's work-life balance but also enhanced his productivity during work hours.

Plan Ahead

Planning ahead is a key strategy for ensuring that personal activities are not overshadowed by work obligations. By scheduling personal activities in advance, you can commit to them and make them a priority in your routine.

Effective Planning Strategies

- **Use a Calendar**: Use a calendar or planner to schedule personal activities, just as you would for work-related tasks. For example, if you want to dedicate time to a hobby, block out time on your calendar, whether it's for a painting class, a weekend hike, or a family movie night. Treat these activities with the same level of importance as work meetings or deadlines. This approach ensures that your personal time is protected and not easily encroached upon by work-related demands.

- **Anticipate and Prepare for Busy Periods**: Life can be unpredictable, and there will be times when work becomes particularly demanding. By planning ahead, you can anticipate these busy periods and adjust your schedule accordingly. For instance, if you know that a big project is coming up at work, you might plan your personal activities around this period, ensuring you still make time for relaxation and self-care without compromising your professional responsibilities.

- **Build in Buffer Time**: When planning your schedule, it's important to include buffer time between activities. This helps prevent the stress of rushing from one task to another and allows for unexpected delays or the need for extra time on certain tasks. For example, if you have a meeting that ends at 3:00 PM and a personal appointment at 4:00 PM, try to include a buffer period of 30 minutes in between. This gives you a chance to decompress, prepare, or simply relax.

Example: The Power of Planning Ahead

Lisa, a corporate lawyer, used to feel overwhelmed by her workload and social commitments. She often found herself canceling personal plans due to last-minute work demands. To regain control of her time, Lisa started using a digital planner to schedule both work and personal activities. She blocked out time each weekend for family outings and personal hobbies, and during the week, she allocated time for exercise and relaxation. By planning her activities in advance, Lisa was able to honor her commitments and maintain a healthier work-life balance.

Setting clear boundaries and allocating time for personal activities are essential practices for achieving a sustainable work-life balance. By defining work hours, designating specific workspaces, turning off work notifications, and learning to say no, you create a framework that protects your time and energy.

Additionally, by implementing time blocking, prioritizing self-care, adopting flexible scheduling, and planning ahead, you ensure that personal activities and well-being are not sacrificed in the pursuit of professional success.

These strategies are not only practical but also necessary for maintaining overall well-being. In a world where work demands can easily encroach upon personal time, establishing and maintaining boundaries is a proactive approach to preserving your mental, emotional, and physical health. By taking these steps, you can create a balanced life where both work and personal fulfillment coexist harmoniously, leading to greater satisfaction, productivity, and long-term happiness.

Balancing Professional and Personal Goals

Aligning your career ambitions with personal values and regularly reviewing your goals can help maintain a balanced life.

Aligning Career Ambitions with Personal Values

Your career goals should reflect your personal values and contribute to your overall well-being.

- **Identify Values:** Reflect on your core values and how they align with your career. Consider aspects such as work-life balance, job satisfaction, and personal growth.

- **Set Meaningful Goals:** Ensure your career goals align with your values. This may involve pursuing a role that offers flexibility, working for a company that values employee well-being, or engaging in work that feels fulfilling.

- **Evaluate Job Satisfaction:** Regularly assess your job satisfaction and make changes if necessary. This could involve seeking new opportunities within your current organization or exploring new career paths.

- **Maintain Balance:** Avoid letting career ambitions overshadow personal values. Strive for a balance that allows you to achieve professional success while maintaining personal happiness.

Regularly Reviewing and Adjusting Goals

Regularly reviewing and adjusting your goals ensures they remain relevant and achievable.

- **Set Short- and Long-Term Goals:** Define both short-term and long-term goals for your career and personal life. This helps you stay focused and motivated.

- **Regular Check-Ins:** Schedule regular check-ins, such as monthly or quarterly reviews, to assess your progress and adjust goals as needed.

- **Be Flexible:** Be open to changing your goals based on new experiences, challenges, or shifts in your values. Flexibility allows you to adapt to changing circumstances and stay aligned with your priorities.

- **Celebrate Achievements:** Acknowledge and celebrate your accomplishments, no matter how small. This can boost your motivation and sense of fulfillment.

Scenario: Mark, a project manager, sets a goal to advance to a senior position within two years. However, he realizes this ambition is causing him to neglect his family and personal interests. After reflecting on his values, Mark decides to adjust his goal to focus on achieving a better work-life balance while still pursuing professional growth. He seeks a role that offers flexibility and aligns with his personal values.

Dealing with Setbacks

Setbacks are inevitable, but effective strategies can help you manage them and learn from challenges.

Strategies for Managing Relapses

Relapses into burnout or stress are common, but they can be managed effectively.

- **Recognize Early Signs:** Pay attention to early signs of burnout, such as fatigue, irritability, or decreased productivity. Early recognition allows for timely intervention.

- **Reassess Your Plan:** When experiencing a setback, reassess your work-life balance plan. Identify areas that need adjustment and implement necessary changes.

- **Seek Support:** Reach out to your support network, including family, friends, or a therapist, for guidance and encouragement.

- **Practice Self-Compassion:** Be kind to yourself and avoid self-criticism. Understand that setbacks are part of the journey and provide opportunities for growth.

Learning from Challenges

Challenges can provide valuable lessons that contribute to personal growth and resilience.

- **Reflect on Experiences:** Take time to reflect on what led to the setback and what you can learn from it. This reflection can provide insights for future prevention and improvement.

- **Develop New Strategies:** Use the lessons learned to develop new strategies for managing stress and maintaining balance. This could involve adjusting your goals, seeking additional support, or adopting new coping mechanisms.

- **Stay Positive:** Maintain a positive attitude and focus on the progress you've made rather than the setback itself. This mindset can help you stay motivated and resilient.

Scenario: Rachel, a teacher, experiences a relapse into burnout after taking on additional responsibilities at work. She recognizes the early signs of fatigue and irritability and decides to reassess her work-life balance plan. Rachel reduces her workload, seeks support from a therapist, and practices self-compassion. Through this process, she learns valuable lessons about setting boundaries and managing stress effectively.

Chapter Eight

Real-Life Success Stories

Real-life stories of overcoming burnout and achieving work-life balance offer valuable lessons and inspiration. In this chapter, we will explore individual case studies, organizational success stories, and expert insights and advice from professionals in mental health and work-life balance.

Case Studies of Overcoming Burnout

Personal stories of overcoming burnout provide relatable and actionable insights.

Individual Stories and Lessons Learned

1. **Emily's Journey to Balance**

Emily, a marketing executive, experienced severe burnout after years of long hours and constant pressure to perform. Her physical health deteriorated, and she felt disconnected from her family and friends.

Recognizing the toll it was taking on her life, Emily decided to make significant changes.

- **Steps Taken:**

  - **Therapy and Coaching:** Emily sought professional help from a therapist and a career coach. Therapy helped her understand the underlying issues contributing to her burnout, while coaching provided practical strategies for managing her workload.

  - **Mindfulness and Self-Care:** She incorporated mindfulness practices into her daily routine, such as meditation and yoga. Emily also made time for self-care activities like reading and spending time outdoors.

  - **Setting Boundaries:** Emily learned to set clear boundaries at work, such as not checking emails after hours and delegating tasks when necessary.

- **Lessons Learned:**

  - The importance of seeking professional help when needed.

  - The value of mindfulness and self-care practices in managing stress.

  - The necessity of setting boundaries to protect personal time and energy.

Inspirational Quote: "You cannot pour from an empty cup. Take care of yourself first." – Unknown

2. **John's Realization and Recovery**

John, a software engineer, found himself working late nights and weekends, leaving him exhausted and irritable. The stress affected his relationships and overall happiness. After a health scare, John realized he needed to change his approach to work.

- **Steps Taken:**

- o **Health Focus:** John started prioritizing his physical health by exercising regularly and adopting a healthier diet.

- o **Work Restructuring:** He negotiated a flexible work schedule with his employer, allowing him to balance work and personal commitments better.

- o **Time Management:** John improved his time management skills by using productivity tools and techniques, such as time-blocking and prioritizing tasks.

- **Lessons Learned:**

  - o Health should be a top priority, as it impacts every aspect of life.

  - o Flexible work arrangements can significantly improve work-life balance.

- o Effective time management is crucial for reducing stress and increasing productivity.

Inspirational Quote: "Almost everything will work again if you unplug it for a few minutes, including you." – Anne Lamott

Organizational Success Stories

Organizations that prioritize work-life balance see improvements in employee well-being and productivity.

Companies that Successfully Implemented Work-Life Balance Initiatives

1. **Tech Innovators Inc.**

Tech Innovators Inc., a leading technology company, faced high employee turnover due to burnout. The management decided to implement a comprehensive work-life balance program to address this issue.

- **Initiatives:**

  o **Flexible Work Schedules:** Employees could choose flexible work hours and work remotely.

  o **Wellness Programs:** The company introduced wellness programs, including fitness classes, mental health support, and stress management workshops.

  o **Employee Support:** Tech Innovators provided access to employee assistance programs (EAPs) and regular mental health check-ins.

- **Results:**

  o A significant reduction in employee turnover rates.

  o Improved job satisfaction and morale.

  o Increased productivity and creativity among employees.

2. **Green Earth Solutions**

Green Earth Solutions, an environmental consulting firm, recognized the importance of work-life balance in maintaining employee engagement and performance.

- **Initiatives:**

  - **Compressed Workweeks:** Employees had the option to work longer hours over fewer days, allowing for extended weekends.

  - **Family-Friendly Policies:** The company introduced family-friendly policies, such as paid parental leave and on-site childcare.

  - **Open Communication:** Regular town hall meetings and feedback sessions encouraged open communication and employee involvement in decision-making.

- **Results:**

  - Enhanced employee loyalty and retention.

  - A healthier, more positive work environment.

  - Better work-life integration for employees.

Expert Insights and Advice

Professional insights provide additional guidance on managing burnout and achieving work-life balance.Interviews with Professionals in Mental Health and Work-Life Balance

1. **Dr. Sarah Collins, Psychologist**

- **Key Points:**

  - **Importance of Early Intervention:** Dr. Collins emphasizes the importance of recognizing early signs of burnout and seeking help promptly. She suggests regular mental health check-ins and promoting a culture of openness about mental health in the workplace.

o **Mindfulness Practices:** Dr. Collins advocates for integrating mindfulness practices into daily routines, such as meditation, deep breathing exercises, and mindful walking. These practices help reduce stress and improve focus.

2. **John Matthews, Work-Life Balance Coach**

- **Key Points:**

  o **Work-Life Integration:** Matthews highlights the concept of work-life integration rather than balance. He suggests blending work and personal life in a way that aligns with individual values and priorities.

  o **Setting Realistic Goals:** Matthews advises setting realistic and achievable goals. He recommends regularly reviewing and adjusting these goals to ensure they remain aligned with changing circumstances and personal growth.

Summary Message: Real-life success stories demonstrate that overcoming burnout and achieving work-life balance is possible with the right strategies and support. By learning from these examples and expert insights, you can take practical steps towards a healthier, more fulfilling life.

Chapter Nine

Tools and Resources

Equipping yourself with the right tools and resources is essential for managing stress and achieving work-life balance. This chapter provides a comprehensive list of recommended books and articles, online resources and apps, and workshops and courses.

Recommended Books and Articles

Essential Reading List

1. **"Burnout: The Secret to Unlocking the Stress Cycle" by Emily Nagoski and Amelia Nagoski**

   o This book provides a science-based approach to understanding and managing burnout, with practical strategies for completing the stress cycle and reclaiming your well-being.

2. **"The Happiness Project" by Gretchen Rubin**

   o Rubin's year-long experiment in pursuing happiness offers insights and actionable steps to improve your overall well-being and find joy in everyday life.

3. **"Essentialism: The Disciplined Pursuit of Less" by Greg McKeown**

   o McKeown's book emphasizes the importance of focusing on what truly matters and eliminating unnecessary distractions to achieve a more balanced and fulfilling life.

4. **"The Power of Now: A Guide to Spiritual Enlightenment" by Eckhart Tolle**

   o This classic book on mindfulness and presence provides profound insights into living in the moment and reducing stress through spiritual awareness.

5. **"Atomic Habits: An Easy & Proven Way to Build Good Habits & Break Bad Ones" by James Clear**

   o Clear offers practical advice on how to develop positive habits and make small changes that lead to significant improvements in your life.

Exercise: Choose one book from the list above and dedicate 30 minutes each day to reading it. Reflect on the lessons learned and how you can apply them to your own life.

Online Resources and Apps

Tools for Managing Stress and Work-Life Balance

1. **Headspace**

   o A popular app for mindfulness and meditation, offering guided meditations, sleep aids, and mindfulness exercises to reduce stress and improve focus.

2. **Calm**

   o An app designed to promote relaxation and mental well-being through guided meditations, sleep stories, breathing exercises, and calming music.

3. **Trello**

   o A project management tool that helps you organize tasks, set priorities, and manage your time effectively to maintain a balanced workload.

4. **MyFitnessPal**

   o An app for tracking your nutrition and exercise, helping you maintain a healthy lifestyle and manage stress through physical well-being.

5. **Forest**

   o An app that encourages focus and productivity by planting virtual trees that grow when you stay off your phone and complete tasks.

Exercise: Download one of the apps mentioned above and use it daily for at least two weeks. Track your progress and note any improvements in your stress levels and work-life balance.

Workshops and Courses

Finding Relevant Training and Development Opportunities

1. **Mindfulness-Based Stress Reduction (MBSR) Courses**

    o MBSR programs teach mindfulness meditation and stress reduction techniques to help individuals manage stress and improve their overall well-being.

2. **Time Management Workshops**

- o Workshops focused on improving time management skills can help you prioritize tasks, set realistic goals, and achieve a better work-life balance.

3. **Employee Assistance Programs (EAPs)**

- o Many organizations offer EAPs that provide access to counseling, stress management workshops, and other resources to support employee well-being.

4. **Professional Development Courses**

- o Look for courses that offer training in areas such as leadership, communication, and resilience. These skills can help you manage work-related stress and achieve a balanced life.

5. **Online Learning Platforms**

- o Platforms like Coursera, Udemy, and LinkedIn Learning offer a wide range of courses on topics related to stress management, work-life balance, and personal development.

Exercise: Identify a workshop or course that aligns with your needs and interests. Register for the course and commit to completing it. Reflect on what you learn and how you can apply it to your daily life.

Interactive Tools and Quizzes

Worksheets and Exercises

Work-Life Balance Worksheet

- **Step 1: Assess Your Current Balance**

  - **Work:** How many hours do you spend working each week? How does this affect your personal life?

  - **Personal:** How much time do you dedicate to personal activities and self-care? Are you satisfied with this balance?

- **Step 2: Set Your Priorities**

  - **List Your Top Priorities:** Identify your top 5 priorities in both your professional and personal life.

  - **Align Your Time with Priorities:** Adjust your schedule to ensure your time is aligned with your priorities.

- **Step 3: Create an Action Plan**

  - **Goals:** Set specific, measurable goals for improving your work-life balance.

  - **Actions:** Identify actionable steps to achieve these goals, such as setting boundaries, delegating tasks, and scheduling personal time.

Quizzes and Assessments

Work-Life Balance Quiz

- **Question 1:** How often do you feel overwhelmed by your workload?

    - o **A:** Always

    - o **B:** Often

    - o **C:** Sometimes

    - o **D:** Rarely

- **Question 2:** Do you regularly make time for self-care activities?

    - o **A:** Never

    - o **B:** Rarely

    - o **C:** Sometimes

    - o **D:** Often

- **Question 3:** How well do you manage your time and prioritize tasks?

- o **A:** Poorly

- o **B:** Fairly

- o **C:** Well

- o **D:** Very Well

Assessment:

- **Mostly A's:** You may need to take significant steps to improve your work-life balance. Consider seeking professional help and making immediate changes to your routine.

- **Mostly B's:** You are aware of the need for balance but may struggle to implement it consistently. Focus on setting clear boundaries and prioritizing self-care.

- **Mostly C's:** You have a relatively good balance but could benefit from fine-tuning your strategies and maintaining consistency.

- **Mostly D's:** You have a healthy work-life balance. Continue to maintain your practices and stay mindful of any potential stressors.

Summary Message: Equipping yourself with the right tools and resources is crucial for managing stress and achieving work-life balance. By utilizing the recommended books, online resources, workshops, and interactive tools, you can take practical steps to enhance your well-being and maintain a balanced life.

This chapter has provided comprehensive guidance on real-life success stories and tools and resources for managing stress and achieving work-life balance. By learning from these examples and utilizing the recommended tools, you can take actionable steps towards a healthier, more fulfilling life.

Conclusion

Recap of Key Takeaways

In this book, we have explored various aspects of overcoming burnout and achieving work-life balance. Each chapter provided insights, strategies, and practical solutions to help you manage stress, maintain well-being, and create a balanced life.z1

1. **Understanding Burnout and Its Causes**

   o Burnout is a state of chronic physical and emotional exhaustion, often caused by prolonged stress. Recognizing the signs and understanding the underlying factors are crucial for addressing burnout effectively.

2. **Identifying Personal and Professional Stressors**

   o Personal and professional stressors can significantly impact your well-being. Identifying these stressors allows you to develop targeted strategies for managing them.

o

3. **Developing Healthy Habits and Routines**

   o Healthy habits and routines, such as regular exercise, adequate sleep, and nutritious eating, are fundamental for maintaining physical and mental health. Establishing a consistent daily routine can help reduce stress and improve overall well-being.

4. **Building a Support System**

   o A strong support system, including supportive relationships at work and in your personal life, is essential for overcoming burnout. Seeking professional help, such as therapy or coaching, can provide additional support and guidance.

5. **Creating a Balanced Work Environment**

   o Redesigning your workday, promoting a healthy workplace culture, and setting boundaries are key steps in creating a balanced work environment. These strategies help reduce stress and enhance productivity.

6. **Enhancing Personal Well-Being**

   o Personal well-being can be enhanced through mindfulness practices, pursuing hobbies, and maintaining a healthy lifestyle. These activities help build resilience and improve emotional well-being.

7. **Implementing Work-Life Balance Practices**

   o Creating a work-life balance plan, aligning professional and personal goals, and effectively managing setbacks are essential for sustaining work-life balance. Regularly reviewing and adjusting your plan ensures it remains relevant and effective.

8. **Real-Life Success Stories**

   o Real-life success stories of individuals and organizations overcoming burnout provide valuable lessons and inspiration. Expert insights and advice from professionals offer additional guidance on managing stress and achieving balance.

9. **Tools and Resources**

   o A variety of tools and resources, including recommended books, online resources, workshops, and interactive tools, are available to support your journey towards work-life balance. These resources provide practical strategies and ongoing support.

Encouragement for Ongoing Improvement

Achieving work-life balance is an ongoing process that requires continuous effort and commitment. Here are some key points to keep in mind as you continue your journey:

- **Be Patient and Persistent:** Change takes time. Be patient with yourself and persistent in your efforts to implement the strategies discussed in this book.

- **Regular Self-Assessment:** Periodically assess your progress and make adjustments as needed. Reflect on what is working well and what areas need improvement.

- **Stay Flexible:** Life is dynamic, and your needs and priorities may change over time. Stay flexible and be willing to adapt your strategies to fit new circumstances.

- **Seek Support:** Don't hesitate to seek support from friends, family, colleagues, or professionals. Building and maintaining a strong support system is crucial for ongoing success.

- **Celebrate Successes:** Acknowledge and celebrate your achievements, no matter how small. Recognizing your progress can boost your motivation and reinforce positive behaviors.

Final Thoughts and Next Steps

As we conclude this book, it's important to recognize that overcoming burnout and achieving work-life balance is a deeply personal journey. Everyone's experience is unique, and there is no one-size-fits-all solution. However, the strategies and insights shared in this book can serve as a foundation for creating a healthier, more balanced life.

Next Steps:

1. **Reflect on Your Journey:** Take some time to reflect on what you've learned from this book. Identify the key takeaways that resonate most with you and consider how you can apply them in your daily life.

2. **Create an Action Plan:** Develop a concrete action plan based on the strategies discussed in this book. Set specific, measurable goals for improving your work-life balance and outline the steps you will take to achieve them.

3. **Implement Small Changes:** Start by implementing small, manageable changes. Focus on one or two areas at a time to avoid feeling overwhelmed. Gradually build on these changes as you gain confidence and see progress.

4. **Engage in Continuous Learning:** Continue to educate yourself on topics related to stress management, well-being, and work-life balance. Stay informed about new research, tools, and resources that can support your journey.

5. **Join a Community:** Consider joining a community or support group focused on work-life balance. Sharing your experiences and learning from others can provide valuable support and motivation.

Key Summary

Overcoming burnout and achieving work-life balance is a multifaceted journey that involves understanding your stressors, developing healthy habits, building a support system, and continuously adapting your strategies. This book has provided you with a comprehensive guide to navigate this journey, offering practical solutions, real-life examples, and expert advice.

Remember, the path to work-life balance is not a linear one. There will be challenges and setbacks along the way, but with persistence and the right tools, you can achieve a more balanced and fulfilling life. Stay committed to your well-being, seek support when needed, and celebrate your progress. Your journey towards work-life balance is a testament to your dedication to living a healthier, happier life.

With this book as your guide, you are well-equipped to face the challenges ahead and create a work-life balance that supports your overall well-being and happiness.

About the Author

Michael Raynal is a passionate advocate for mental wellness and personal development. With over a decade of experience in helping individuals overcome burnout and achieve work-life balance, Michael has dedicated his career to empowering others to lead more fulfilling and balanced lives. His insights are rooted in real-world experience, having worked with professionals across various industries who face the daily challenges of stress, overwork, and exhaustion.

Drawing from his extensive background in stress management, mindfulness, and productivity enhancement, Michael has crafted a series of practical and transformative guides that have resonated with readers around the world. His work is driven by a deep commitment to making mental wellness accessible to everyone, offering actionable strategies that can be seamlessly integrated into everyday life.

Michael's approach is both compassionate and pragmatic, reflecting his belief that everyone has the potential to overcome burnout and reclaim their life with the right tools and mindset. As a bestselling author, he continues to inspire and guide readers on their journey toward a healthier, more balanced life.

When he's not writing, Michael enjoys spending time with his family, practicing meditation, and exploring new ways to live a balanced and mindful life. His mission is simple: to help as many people as possible find the peace, purpose, and productivity they deserve.